OPEN ROAD'S BEST OF

Arizona

by Becky Youman

Open Road Travel Guides – designed for the
amount of time you *really* have for your trip!

Arizona

To my traveling partners – Bryan and Sierra

Text Copyright © 2006 by Becky Youman
- All Rights Reserved -
ISBN 1-59360-084-4
Library of Congress Control No. 2006929091

Maps by designmaps.com. Photos © ShutterStock.com, except on pages 13, 14, 29, 60, 147 and 150 © Scottsdale Convention & Visitors Bureau and page 124 © Becky Youman. Note: some material in this book comes from Open Road Publishing's *Arizona Guide* by Larry Ludmer. The author has made every effort to be as accurate as possible, but neither she nor the publisher assumes responsibility for the services provided by any business listed in this guide; for any errors or omissions; or any loss, damage, or disruptions in your travels for any reason.

CONTENTS

Your Passport to the **Perfect Trip!**

Maps

Open Road's
BEST OF ARIZONA

1. INTRODUCTION

Arizona's **natural wonders** – from the vast expanse of the **Grand Canyon** to the strange and fiery **red rocks of Sedona** to the surreal forests of fifty foot high **Saguaro cactus** – are unparalleled in the country. Every part of the state is filled with amazing physical landscapes that showcase what nature offers. These range from wildflower-dotted deserts to lush alpine forests. Add to that the fascinating influence of both Native American and Hispanic cultures and you've got a destination that is truly unique in terms of scenery, history, architecture, and cuisine.

This book will guide you to the **best of the best**, be it lodging, restaurants, or attractions. Whether you desire a break at one of the world's greatest full service luxury resorts or prefer a relaxing stay at a historic railroad inn, Arizona's got it and this book will take you there. We offer five-star southwestern cuisine prepared using classic French methods as well as shacks serving up Navajo tacos and fry-bread. We'll also give you the full run-down on the state's most popular attractions as well as lead you to others that might not get as much press but are truly worthy of a visit.

This guide covers **all the information you need** to plan day trips, short weekend jaunts or longer trips through beautiful Arizona without burdening you with long lists and options that simply aren't worth your precious vacation time. Just take off and enjoy – you've got a great trip ahead!

2. OVERVIEW

Arizona's abundant natural beauty is no secret, but that's only part of the story. The state enjoys a unique ethos that results from a **mosaic of cultural influences**. Both the **Hispanic** (in the form of Spanish and Mexican traditions) and the **Native American** impacts are strong. In fact, almost the entire northeastern quarter of the state is occupied by Indian reservations, especially those of the Navajo and Hopi.

The **"Old West" influence** still survives in Arizona's populace, despite the influx of people from all over the country. In many things, from politics to such mundane issues as Daylight Savings Time, Arizonians forge their own path.

To make planning your trip easier, this book has been divided into **seven different touring regions**. The remainder of this chapter will briefly describe each of the regions and suggest a few itineraries.

Phoenix
The state's **capital and largest city**, Phoenix is also Arizona's economic, cultural and recreational heart. **Centrally located**, it is a good spot for reaching out into almost every other part of the state as well as the logical arrival point for visitors coming in by air.

A modern city with fine museums and numerous cultural attractions, greater Phoenix, also called The Valley, is home to more than a dozen world-class **luxury resorts** and numerous fine dining establishments. **Progressive and vibrant**, Phoenix has something for everyone and is within easy reach of many scenic attractions.

Tucson
Smaller than Phoenix, Tucson retains a greater Hispanic and Native American presence than its more cosmopolitan sister to the north. That influence, along with the fine museums and University of Arizona, combine to give Tucson a **rich cultural life**. Luxury resorts abound, as do some of the state's best **guest ranches**. Day trips to Mexico and Old West towns like **Tombstone and Bisbee** are popular diversions for many Tucson visitors.

North-Central Arizona
Comprised of Sedona, Flagstaff, Prescott, and Jerome, this region is incredible. Located almost entirely within a series of national forests, it's one of the **best areas in the state for outdoor recreation**.

Flagstaff is a gateway to the **Grand Canyon**, as well as a central location for visiting several fascinating national monuments that feature unusual geological phenomena and the remains of ancient civilizations. It's also got the best snow skiing in the state. Yes, there are **pine-covered mountains** in Arizona.

Arizona's Best!

Given a limited amount of vacation time, you should try and do as many of these as your schedule will permit:

- **Grand Canyon** – Northwestern Arizona
- **Red Rocks of Sedona** – North-Central Arizona
- **Sunset Crater-Wupatki Loop** – near Flagstaff, North-Central Arizona
- **Monument Valley** – Northeastern Arizona
- **Canyon de Chelly** – Northeastern Arizona
- **Sonoran Desert** – Tucson
- **Scottsdale Resorts, Night on the Town** – Phoenix

The picturesque artist's community of **Sedona** is home to the **famous red rocks** of Oak Creek Canyon and numerous recreational opportunities. **Prescott and Jerome**, with rich histories of cowboys and miners, both hearken back to the days of the **Wild West**.

Grand Canyon

You could take a week in Arizona and visit only the Grand Canyon. You can opt for the easy way and see it only from the rim; or be more adventurous and **hike** or take a **mule ride** down into the canyon. Or maybe you want to see it from the air or from a **raft** on the Colorado River.

The **possibilities are endless** and no matter how little or much time you have, the experience will be a rewarding one.

Northeastern Arizona

The Navajo Indian Reservation is the largest in the United States. It completely surrounds the smaller Hopi Reservation. Together they comprise almost the entire northeastern portion of Arizona. Many areas are open to the public and you can learn much about the **Navajo and Hopi cultures**. Scenery and history also abound in this region with **outstanding ruins, canyons, and monolithic rock formations**.

Eastern Arizona

This **mountainous region**, a haven for the desert-dwellers of Phoenix and Tucson, is little known outside the state. You'll find the scenic **Mogollon Rim** and the beautiful **White Mountains**, which are perfect for a cool-weather getaway.

Western Arizona

This area is the least developed in terms of both population and tourist facilities. Along the western border of the state however (the Colorado River), there are numerous recreation and resort options. There's **Lake Havasu**, with the original London Bridge, as well as Bullhead City, just across the river from the gambling town of **Laughlin, Nevada**. Don't forget **Kingman**, with its Route 66 roots, and **Wickenburg**, home of numerous dude ranches.

Itineraries

If you've never been to Arizona before, you'll want to make sure you hit the highlights. If all you've got is a weekend, you should cover both the amazing vistas of the **Grand Canyon** and the red rocks of **Sedona**, stopping at the cliff dwellings of **Montezuma National Monument** on your way back to Phoenix.

If you've got a week, you can fit in Sedona, Flagstaff and its surrounding monuments, the Grand Canyon, Canyon de Chelly, Monument Valley and the Navajo National Monument. You might even have time for some R&R in Scottsdale.

Each destination chapter of the book points out the best sights in that region, so another option is to just pick out those that sound interesting and make up the perfect itinerary for you.

3. PHOENIX & SCOTTSDALE

Greater Phoenix, otherwise known as "The Valley," is a thriving and fast-growing metropolis surrounded by arid mountains and blessed with an average of 300 sunny days a year. In the heart of the Valley is Phoenix proper, where you'll find many cultural activities, excellent restaurants, and a reinvigorated downtown that is home to a number of professional sports teams.

Just to the east is Scottsdale, the epicenter of the Valley's luxury resorts and golf courses. Museums and restaurants catering to both the well-heeled and the hip abound here. South of Scottsdale you'll find collegiate Tempe, home to the Sun Devils of Arizona State University. Scottsdale and Tempe, along with the cities of Mesa and Chandler, are often referred to as the "East Valley." The West Valley includes the city of Glendale, new home to the Arizona Cardinals NFL team.

ONE GREAT DAY IN PHOENIX

With only one day in Phoenix, you'll want to get a taste of both the southwestern and resort influences that flavor the Valley. Visit the Heard Museum, take a breather at the Frank Lloyd Wright inspired Biltmore Resort, and then stroll among thousands of cactus at the Desert Botanical Garden. After that explore the shops and galleries of Old Town Scottsdale before dining at one of the many five-star options nearby.

If you find yourself up early, fuel up before starting your day at My Florist Café (see *Phoenix Sleeps & Eats*) for a delicious taste of "hip" Phoenix. It's not far from your first stop.

After breakfast, make a beeline for the Heard Museum, one of the world's most outstanding collections of southwestern art and culture. Upon arrival at the gorgeous Spanish Colonial building, ask if there are any live demonstrations. Often Native Americans are on hand to discuss their artistic techniques while they work, something you won't want to forego.

With over 35,000 Native American objects in seven different galleries, the Heard simply has more displays than you can take in. Focus on the HOME: Native People of the Southwest gallery, an interactive exhibit that chronicles the cultures of America's Indians. Don't miss the Navajo hogan and the Hopi piki room. *Info*: 2103 N Central Ave. Tel. 602-252-8848. www.heard.org. Open daily 9:30am-5:00pm. Admission: $10 adults, $3 children 6-12.

From the Heard, jump in your car and head eight miles northeast to lunch at the Arizona Biltmore and Villas. Influenced by the famous architect Frank Lloyd Wright and built in the 1920s, the Arizona Biltmore was the first of the Phoenix area's modern luxury resorts. The Wright style is notable for its harmonious mixture of building and natural surroundings, which you'll

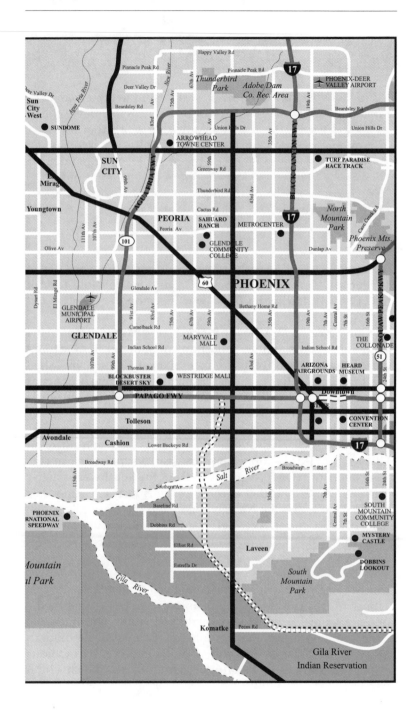

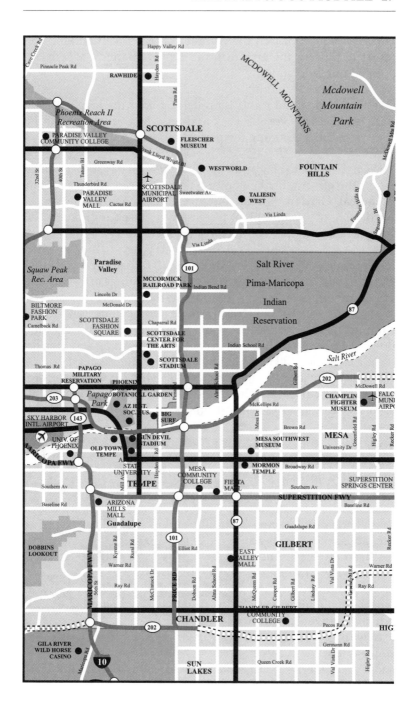

notice as you approach the complex. Take a walk around the resort to admire the architectural details, many of which are pointed out by plaques.

Don't eat inside, but rather sit outside under the loggia at **The Café** (see *Phoenix Sleeps & Eats*) and relax as you look out at the colorful gardens framing the perfect mountain vista.

You might want to stay and enjoy the view all day, but it will be worth the effort to make your next stop the remarkable **Desert Botanical Garden**. Spread out over 145 acres, the Botanical Garden has over 20,000 plant specimens representing about 4,000 species native to the world's most arid climates.

Head straight to the **Desert Discovery Trail**, a brick path that winds a third of a mile through the oldest plantings in the garden. The strange, quiet beauty of these plants that survive the harshest of elements will undoubtedly surprise and intrigue you. (In the summer months you might want to switch it up and visit the Botanical Garden in the relative cool of the morning and then hit the air-conditioned Heard in the heat of the afternoon.) *Info:* 2101 N Galvin Parkway in Papago Park. Tel. 480-941-1225. www.dbg.org. Open daily October though April 8am-8pm; May-September 7am-8pm. Admission: $10 adults, $4 children 3-12.

Your next stop, a ten-minute drive northeast, is the **Scottsdale Arts District**, where you'll find a concentration of outstanding galleries. If contemporary art is your style, head to **Marshall Way**, where you can view cutting edge work from around the world. If you prefer western and Native American art, walk a few blocks south to the **Main Street** shops and galleries. *Info:* Located between Fifth Avenue and Main

ALTERNATIVE PLAN: Not a museum aficionado? Check out the local paper to see what's happening at **Arizona State University** in Tempe. There may be a sporting or cultural event of interest. If sports are your thing, be sure the check the schedules of the Diamondbacks, Cardinals, and the **other professional teams** that make their homes in the valley as well (see *Phoenix Best Activities*).

Downtown Phoenix

Street in Old Town Scottsdale. Tel. Scottsdale Gallery Association 480-990-3939. www.scottsdalegalleries.com.

Finish up your evening at **Cowboy Ciao**, one of the many outstanding restaurants in Old Town. A whimsical marriage of Italy and the Old West, Cowboy Ciao features Modern American food and one of the largest wine lists in the country. After dinner, if you're still raring to go, ask the hostess to point you to the unmarked door that leads to the **Kazbar**, a swank speak-easy with live music (see *Phoenix Nightlife*).

A FANSTASTIC PHOENIX WEEKEND

Take gourmet restaurants, lush resorts, interesting museums and historic architecture – mix with beautiful desert scenery and toney galleries – and you've got the ingredients for a great weekend in the Valley of the Sun.

Friday Evening

Head straight to the **Arizona Biltmore and Villas** to seep yourself in the Phoenix vibe and enjoy a relaxing outdoor drink before dinner. The first of the Valley's modern luxury resorts, the Biltmore was influenced by famous architect Frank Lloyd Wright. You'll notice the Wright style, a harmonious meshing of buildings and natural surroundings, from the moment you arrive at the property. Stretch your traveling legs by walking around the resort to admire the many architectural details.

After your stroll, ignore the hotel's indoor restaurants to grab one of the outdoor sofas under the loggia at the **Squaw Peak Lounge** (see *Phoenix Sleeps & Eats*). It's one of the best spots on the city to look out at the mountains in the background while enjoying perfectly manicured gardens and melodious fountains in the foreground.

From there you'll take a ten minute drive through the heart of the Camelback Corridor shopping and eating district on your way to **Arcadia**, one of the most desired addresses in the city. Rambling homes on large citrus-covered lots remind visitors of a pre-McMansion Phoenix. At the intersection of 40th streets and Campbell you'll find two excellent restaurants. Check out the contemporary vibe and well-stocked shelves of **La Grande Orange Grocery and Pizzeria** before walking over to the outstanding **Postino Winecafe** for dinner (see *Phoenix Sleeps & Eats*). After dinner, head to **Old Town Scottsdale** for nightlife galore. Try the **Zuzu Lounge** at the Hotel Valley Ho for a super cool late night scene.

Saturday

You'll spend your morning in Central Phoenix at the world-renown **Heard Museum**. Housing an amazing collection of southwestern art and culture, the museum has over 35,000 objects on display in the fantastic Spanish Colonial-style building. Inquire when buying tickets if there are any **live demonstrations**, which feature native artisans explaining their techniques while they work.

ALTERNATIVE PLAN: If you're looking for upscale elegance instead of the hip Phoenix scene, dine at the nearby **Vincent's on Camelback**. If romance and luxury are your intended outcomes, you can't beat **T. Cooks** at the Royal Palms Hotel for an unforgettable dining experience (see *Phoenix Sleeps & Eats*).

Begin your visit at the **HOME: Native People of the Southwest** gallery. This interactive and highly interesting exhibit focuses on the native cultures of the region. Don't miss the Navajo hogan and the Hopi piki room. From there, if you still have museum stamina, move on to the **Every Picture Tells a Story** gallery where craft activities and take-home projects encourage you to get "hands on." *Info:* 2103 N Central Ave. Tel. 602-252-8848. www.heard.org. Open daily 9:30am-5:00pm. Admission: $10 adults, $3 children 6-12.

You'll have lunch at the nearby **My Florist Café**, a hip restaurant in a converted flower shop (see *Phoenix Sleeps & Eats*). After your meal, take some digestion time to admire the impeccably re-stored Tudor, Spanish Revival and Bungalow homes in the adjacent **Willo historic district**. Start by foot or car at 3rd Avenue and McDowell and head north to Thomas and west to 7th Avenue.

After your tour, drive south on 7th Street to downtown Phoenix's **Heritage Square**. The square is home to the only remaining group of residential structures from the original Phoenix town site. Although all eight of the buildings on the site have historical significance, the most interesting one to tour is the **Rosson House**, a Victorian mansion built in 1895 by the mayor of Phoenix. *Info:* 115 N 6th St. Tel. 602-262-5029. www.phoenix.gov/PARKS/heritage.html. Wednesday-Saturday 10am-3:30pm. Sunday noon-3:30pm. Admission: $4 adults, $1 children 6-12.

After touring the Rosson House, pop into the **Phoenix Museum of History** across the square to immerse yourself in the city's past. Focus on the **Main Gallery** with, among other things, a reproduction of "lunger tents", once home to recovering TB sufferers. *Info:* Tel. 105 N. 5th St. 602-253-2734. www.pmoh.org. Tuesday-Saturday 10am-5pm. Admission: $6 adults, $3 children 7-12.

After visiting the museum, walk back across the square to the Baird Machine Shop, now the home of **Pizzeria Bianco**. Put your name on the waiting list (there always is one, but believe me the pizza is worth it), and head next door to the Thomas House, which houses the Bar Bianco (see *Phoenix Sleeps & Eats*). Order a drink and enjoy the wait as you sit outside surrounded by remnants of the Valley's past.

Sunday
Begin your morning with a tour of the remarkable **Desert Botanical Garden**, 145 acres of plant species from the world's deserts. Start on the paved **Desert Discovery Trail**, lined with the oldest plantings in the garden. You'll be amazed at the strange beauty of cacti and succulents. Be sure to veer off onto the **Sonoran Desert Nature Trail** to enjoy the view through the telescopes at the Mountain Vista point. *Info:* 2101 NGalvin Parkway in Papago Park. Tel. 480-941-1225. www.dbg.org.

Open daily October though April 8am-8pm; May-September 7am-8pm. Admission: $10 adults, $4 children 3-12.

After your tour of the garden, drive northeast to the **Scottsdale Civic Center Mall**. Featuring live music and art shows many weekends of the year, the mall (in the sense of "open public space" not "shopping center")

ALTERNATIVE PLAN: Not a big fan of museums? Take advantage of the **awesome outdoor activities** Phoenix has to offer. Try golf at one of the **Valley's famous courses** or a hike at one of the city's many **desert wilderness parks** (see *Phoenix Best Activities*).

is a delightful maze of lush gardens, ponds, fountains and sculptures. It's best just to meander through the plaza, but don't miss a photo op at the **Robert Indiana "Love" Sculpture** of postal stamp fame. *Info:* 3939 N. Drinkwater Boulevard. Tel. 480-874-4607.

Stop for lunch at **The Restaurant**, in the Mondrian Hotel right on the main plaza (see Phoenix Sleeps & Eats), before checking out the **Scottsdale Museum of Contemporary Art**, also on the grounds of the Civic Center Mall. Manageably small, you can easily tour the three galleries in under an hour. *Info:* 7374 East Second Street. Tel. 480-994-ARTS. www.smoca.org. Open Tuesday-Saturday 10am-5pm. (open until 8pm Thursdays) Sunday noon-5pm. Admission: $7 adults, children under 15 free. Free on Thursdays.

ALTERNATIVE PLAN: If you want to get out and burn some calories after all the great food you've had this weekend, you should walk, bike, or skate along the paved **Indian Bend Wash Greenbelt** in Scottsdale. Connecting multiple parks and golf courses, the greenbelt offers miles of car-free paths (see *Phoenix Best Activities*).

If you're hungry for dessert, walk over to Scottsdale Road and pop into the **Sugar Bowl**, a local institution that you might recognize from Family Circus cartoons (4005 N Scottsdale Road, Scottsdale and Main). From there, saunter to the shops and galleries of the **Scottsdale Arts District**. Focus on the galleries of **Marshall Way** if you prefer contemporary art, or those on **Main Street** for western and Native American works. *Info:* Located between Fifth Avenue and Main Street in Old Town Scottsdale. Tel. Scottsdale Gallery Association 480-990-3939. www.scottsdalegalleries.com.

After you have gallery hopped to your heart's content, walk across the canal on the Soleri designed **Sun Dial Bridge** to the recently developed **Scottsdale Waterfront**. Created to connect Old Town Scottsdale with **Scottsdale Fashion Square**, the Waterfront is home to both retail shopping and fine dining establishments. End your weekend with dinner at the Waterfront at either the upscale **Eddie V's Wildfish Seafood Grille** or the casual and somewhat raucous Vegas import the **Pink Taco** (see *Phoenix Best Activities*).

A WEEK IN THE VALLEY OF THE SUN

With a week in Phoenix there's time to do it all – you'll visit fabulous museums and Indian ruins, commune with nature and take in the stunning southwestern landscapes. When you get hungry, dine in style at one of my favorite restaurants in the Phoenix section of the *Sleeps & Eats* chapter.

RECOMMENDED PLAN: Take a day each for the Phoenix and Scottsdale downtown areas. Use another couple of days to explore Taliesin West, the Desert Botanical Garden, and spend some good time outdoors. Choose two other days for unique drives to impressive ruins and old mining towns, and don't forget a day to enjoy Tempe and ASU.

Downtown Phoenix
If you are at all interested in Native American culture, head to one of the world's finest collections of southwestern art and culture at the **Heard Museum**. The Heard is so big you can't

possibly take it all in, so focus on the best of the best –
the **HOME: Native People
of the Southwest gallery.**
This interactive exhibit
chronicles the cultures of
American's Indians with
fascinating displays like a
Navajo hogan and Hopi piki
room.

When buying your tickets
ask if there are any **live demonstrations**. The museum
often features native artisan

Don't Miss...

• **The Heard Museum** – Amazing Native American culture
• **The Desert Botanical Garden**
  – More interesting cacti than
  you could ever imagine
• **Old Town Scottsdale** – Fine
  arts and fine nightlife
• **Frank Lloyd Wright's Legacy**
  – at either the Arizona Biltmore
  or Taliesin West

discussing their techniques as they work. *Info:* 2103 N Central Ave.
Tel. 602-252-8848. www.heard.org. Open daily 9:30am-5:00pm.
Admission: $10 adults, $3 children 6-12.

After visiting the museum, it's worth taking some time to tour the
impeccably restored Tudor, Spanish Revival and Bungalow homes
in the adjacent **Willo historic district**. Start by foot or car at 3rd
Avenue and McDowell and head north to Thomas and west to
7th Avenue.

A few blocks east is the **Phoenix Art Museum**. If you're interested in any of the exhibits, many of which are world class, by all
means take your time and enjoy. The temporary exhibits on the
first floor are usually what draw me to the museum. A good place
for a nice, casual lunch is the **Museum Café by Arcadia Farms**.
(You don't have to pay to enter the museum if all you're doing is
eating lunch.) *Info:* 1625 N. Central Avenue. Tel. 602-257-1222.
Open Tuesday-Sunday, 10am to 5pm (Open until 9pm on Thursdays.) Admission: $9 adults, $3 children 6-17.

Just down the street is the **Burton Barr Central Library**. Yes, that's
right – the library. It's totally worth a stop. The futuristic architecture is unique among Phoenix public buildings and is complemented by state-of-the-art technology inside. Computers run large
blinds and sails that open and close to regulate the amount of

sunlight coming into the building. *Info:* 1221 N. Central Ave. Tel. 602-262-4636. www.phoenixpubliclibrary.org. Open Monday-Thursday 10am-9pm, Friday-Saturday 10am-6pm, and Sunday noon-6pm. Free admission.

South of the library, on the other side of I-10, you'll find downtown Phoenix's historic **Heritage Square**. There's not much left of the original Phoenix town site, but eight of the city's residential structures have been restored here. Be sure to tour the **Rosson House**, a Victorian mansion built by the city's mayor in 1895, for a look at how the Rich & Famous lived back in the day. *Info:* 115 N 6th St. Tel. 602-262-5029. www.phoenix.gov/PARKS/heritage.html. Wednesday-Saturday 10am-3:30pm. Sunday noon-3:30pm. Admission: $4 adults, $1 children 6-12.

Another nearby museum, across the square, is the **Phoenix Museum of History**. Focus on the **Main Gallery** with, among other things, a reproduction of "lunger tents", once home to recovering TB sufferers. *Info:* Tel. 105 N. 5th St. 602-253-2734. www.pmoh.org. Tuesday-Saturday 10am-5pm. Admission: $6 adults, $3 children 7-12.

Scottsdale

Scottsdale and the fine arts make a well-matched couple. Start at the **Scottsdale Civic Center Mall**. (This is a "mall" in the sense of "open public space" not a shopping center") Spend some time wandering the delightful maze of lush gardens, ponds, fountains and sculptures. Be sure to stop for a photo at the **Robert Indiana "Love" Sculpture**, which you've probably seen on postage stamps.

Downtown for Dinner?

I suggested Pizzeria and Bar Bianco in the weekend plan if you're downtown, but Cibo at 5th Ave and Fillmore is another great choice. With a more urban vibe, Cibo offers up fantastic hand-tossed pizza and organic produce in a beautifully restored home in the Roosevelt Historic District. Tel. 602-441-2697.

On one side of the plaza, just beyond the Performing Arts Center, you'll find the edgy **Scottsdale Museum of Contemporary Art**.

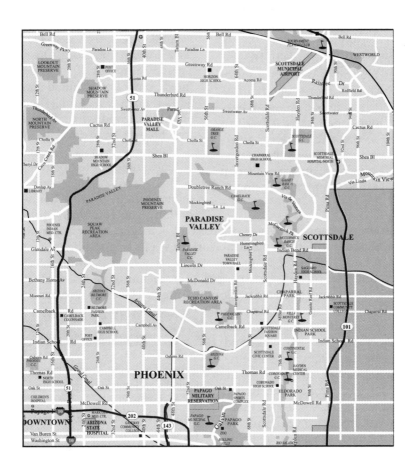

Lunch and a Show

Enjoy lunch indoors or out at **AZ88** (see *Phoenix Sleeps & Eats*), one of the most popular restaurants on the mall. You might even catch a live performance. The restaurant is right in front of the outdoor stage that features music many weekends and **Native American** dance and music performances Tuesday, Thursdays, and Saturdays at noon in the winter and spring.

With a wide variety of ever-changing exhibits, the museum explores modern culture through art and architecture. Manageably small, you can easily tour the three galleries in under an hour. *Info:* 7374 East Second Street. Tel. 480-994-ARTS. www.smoca.org. Open Tuesday-Saturday 10am-5pm. (open until 8pm Thursdays) Sunday noon-5pm. Admission: $7 adults, children under 15 free. Free on Thursdays.

A ten-minute drive north on Scottsdale road is the bizarre, otherworldly **Cosanti Foundation**. The founder, Paolo Soleri, defines his work as arcology – a type of architecture integrated with the ecological workings of its surroundings. You can tour earthformed concrete structures amid a natural desert setting that includes cactus, palo verde, and olive trees. Most interesting are the **cause bells**, which are cast bronze and ceramic wind chimes made in honor of various worthy causes around the world. Take one home and enjoy the unique tones as a reminder of your trip to Arizona. *Info:* 6433 Doubletree Ranch Road. Tel. 480-948-6145. www.arcosanti.org. Open 9am-5pm daily. No admission fee.

Art Walk

Every Thursday from 7pm-9pm the galleries stay open late for **Art Walk**, an open-house of sorts where you can tour the galleries, learn about the artists, and talk to gallery owners. *Info:* Between Fifth Avenue and Main Street in Old Town Scottsdale. Tel. 480-990-3939, www.scottsdalegalleries.com.

Scottsdale is known for its world-class **spas**, so what better way to enjoy your time here than getting pampered at one of the luxury resorts in town. Even if you're not staying at the resorts, you can enjoy their spa packages and many times have access to their swimming

The Grand Canyon
at sunset

Havasu Falls

Home with
Saguaro cactus

Montezuma Cliff Dwellings

Sedona's famous
Red Rocks

Monument Valley

Apache Lake along the Apache Trail, near Phoenix

Saguaro National Forest, Tucson

pools and other facilities. Some of the best pampering can be found at the **Fairmont Princess**, the **Hyatt Gainey**, and **The Phoenician** (see *Phoenix Sleeps & Eats*).

The **Scottsdale Arts District**, right in the heart of Old Town, is well worth your time if you're an art lover. Focus on the galleries of **Marshall Way** if you prefer contemporary art, or those on **Main Street** for western and Native American works. Don't miss the Soleri designed **Sun Dial Bridge** that crosses the canal on Marshall Way.

About twenty minutes northeast of downtown Scottsdale you can visit **Frank Lloyd Wright's** remarkable **Taliesin West**. Wright, arguably one of the most important architects in American history, established a winter "camp" in Scottsdale in 1937 for his apprentices. He and his charges literally created Taliesin West out of the desert by collecting rocks and sand for the construction of a complex of buildings that served as his personal home, studio and architectural campus until his death in 1959.

There are a variety of tour options, but first-time visitors should take the one-hour **Panoramic Tour**. Guides explain how the architecture relates to the desert and provide a general overview of Wright's basic design theories. It's amazing to see how each building and outdoor space was very purposely constructed to illustrate his ideas. *Info:* Located at Cactus Road and Frank Lloyd Wright Boulevard. Tel. 480-860-2700. www.franklloydwright.org. Open daily 9am-4pm. Tour prices vary from $18 to $45 for adults and $5-$15 for children 4-12.

Tempe

The main event in Tempe is **Arizona State University**. (ASU is just south of the 202 and west of the 101 along the Rio Salado.) The first thing you should do is check the paper for a sporting or cultural event that piques your interest.

Start your tour at Rural and Apache at the Visitor Information Center to get a map of the recommended walking tour. Don't miss the **Gammage Auditorium**, Frank Lloyd Wright's last public structure; and the **Arizona State University Art Museum**, with an excellent collection of American and European works. You'll also want to saunter down the school's main drag, **Mill Avenue**, to get a sense of the current college scene.

The Mall of Good Eats!

About ten minutes west of Taliesin is Kierland Commons, a bucolic open-air shopping mall with a number of wonderful eateries. Try Zinc, an excellent Parisian bistro complete with a real zinc bar; North, specializing in modern Italian dishes, or The News Café for fast, casual fare. Don't miss the Valley's own Cold Stone Creamery for dessert.

**Apache Trail &
Tonto National Monument**
The nearby **Apache Trail** is one of the **most beautiful drives in the state**. Built in 1905 during the construction of the Roosevelt Dam, the route closely follows the path once taken by the Apache Indians as they traveled through the canyons of the Salt River. You'll experience outstanding mountain, lake, and desert scenery as well as historic towns and ruins over the course of the 190-mile drive. To get there, follow US60 east of town to AZ88 and the town of **Apache Junction**.

Tempe's Best Meal

Before or after your chosen sporting or cultural event, make it a priority to have either a drink or meal at the nearby House of Tricks, the best and most pleasant restaurant in Tempe (see *Phoenix Sleeps & Eats*).

Continue on AZ88 into the heart of the scenic views (and the curves). Several beautiful lakes link together like a chain of pearls across the collarbones of the Superstitions. You can stop for a 90-minute tour of **Canyon Lake** on **The Dolly Steamboat**, but if you do you might not have time to view the rest of the attractions on the loop in one day. *Info:* Canyon Lake Marina and Campground. Tel. 480-827-91444. www.dollysteamboat.com. Daily 12pm and 2pm. $17 adults, $9.50 children 6-12.

Lost Dutchman Hike

You will reach a stretch, just past **Tortilla Flat**, where you have 26-miles of unpaved road. Just take it slowly and you'll be fine. The highlight here is **Fish Creek Canyon** with its **2,000-foot high multicolored walls**. The road returns to pavement at the impressive **Roosevelt Dam**. Four miles beyond the dam is the very worthwhile **Tonto National Monument**. A well-preserved, **two-story cliff dwelling** that dates from the 14th century, the ruins were built into a natural cave about 350 feet above the visitor's center by the Salado Indians. There is a steep, paved one-mile roundtrip trail to the lower cliff dwelling that you can visit on your own. Guided hikes to the upper dwelling must be reserved in advance, take three hours, and involve a three-mile hike. You can also just enjoy the view of the dwelling from below. Many of the objects recovered from the dwellings can be seen in the visitor's center museum. *Info:* Four miles east of Roosevelt Dam on AZ88. Tel. 928-467-2241. www.nps.gov/tont/index.htm. Open daily 8am-5pm. Admission $4 per vehicle.

There are some excellent hikes in the Superstition Mountains that loom to the east. They are best accessed through the nearby Lost Dutchman State Park, so you should stop for a scramble if you are so inclined. *Info:* 6109 N. Apache Trail. Tel. 480-982-4485. Open daily sunrise to 10pm. Admission $5 per vehicle.

The final 28 miles of the Apache Trail are a much easier drive than the first part of the trip. You've got another chance to walk through a Salado Indian pueblo at the **Besh-Ba-Gowah Archaeological Park**, where some of the dwellings have been restored and furnished. You even get to climb ladders to the upper stories of the dwelling if you'd like. There is also an interesting museum that documents Salado life in the 13th century. *Info:* South of Globe off of US60. Tel. 928-425-0320. Open daily 9am-5pm. Admission $2.

Lunch in Globe

Globe, a historic mining town, is a good option for a late lunch. The city was supposedly named after a globe-shaped piece of silver found nearby. Exit on Broad to downtown Globe and stop at La Casita Café for a memorable taste of Mother Salustia Reynosa's original recipes. The cheese crisp is classic Arizona-Mex and the enchiladas are fantastic. Tel 928-425-8462.

Heading back towards Phoenix on US60 is the stunning **Devil's Canyon**, characterized by very jagged and rocky ridges and unusual pointed formations. Three miles west of Superior the **Boyce Thompson Southwest Arboretum** is tucked into the base of Picketpost Mountain. A staggering variety of desert vegetation has been gathered from all over the world and is beautifully planted on the Arboretum's 420 acres. The easy paths that meander through the property cover desert terrain as well as areas with an unexpected amount of dense vegetation home to numerous colorful birds. *Info:* US60 milepost 223. Tel. 520-689-2811. http://arboretum.ag.arizona.edu. Open daily in summer 6am-3pm and 8am-4pm the rest of the year. Admission $7.50 adults, $3.00 children 5-12.

Jump back on US60 and you'll return to the Valley in about 45-minutes.

Historic Florence & Casa Grande Ruins National Monument
Get a taste of both western and Native American cultures in an easy drive from metro Phoenix.

Head south on I-10 to exit 185 and follow the signs east to the **Casa Grande Ruins National Monument**. (Do not follow the signs to the town of Casa Grande.) Casa Grande was the first archeological site to be preserved by the federal government. Meaning the "Big House," Casa Grande was constructed around 1350 by the **Hohokam Indians**. The settlement was abandoned approximately a hundred years after it was built for reasons unknown.

Casa Grande is of great historical importance because it represents the ultimate architectural achievement of Hohokam society. The monument consists of a large central structure that is four stories high and built out of layers of mud. This is surrounded by the remains of a walled village. You can take either a self-guided or ranger-conducted walk through the ruins. It will take about an hour to tour the monument and visit the on-site museum. *Info:* AZ87. Tel. 520-723-3172. www.nps.gov/cagr/index.htm. Open daily 8am-5pm. Admission $5 adults, children under 15 free.

From Casa Grande, take AZ287 to **Florence**, an old west town that has retained much of its historic flavor. There are over 150 buildings here that are on the National Register of Historic Places. Take the time to walk down Main Street and you'll feel like you have walked back in time. (Main and 8th Ave.)

If you're interested in the history of the area, stop at the excellent **Pinal County Historical Museum** at 715 S. Main. It's small, but has many interesting items such as buckskin playing cards and beautiful furniture crafted from cholla and saguaro cactus. If you're up for more history, you can also tour the **McFarland State Historic Park** in the former county courthouse, at the other end of Main.

For lunch, head straight across the street from the Pinal Country Museum to the **LB Inn** at 695 S Main for some **simple but delicious Mexican food**. (They also serve burgers and sandwiches.) If it's a nice day request a table by the fountain on the large back patio and order up the daily special.

The Great Outdoors
Many people are drawn to Phoenix for the weather – so you need to get outside and enjoy it!

The remarkable **Desert Botanical Garden** is a must-see. Spread tanical Garden has 20,000 plant specimens representing about 4,000 species native to the world's out over 145 acres, the Bomost arid climates. The **Discovery Trail**, a brick path that winds through the oldest plantings in the garden, is a good place to start. Ask when you enter if any wild-

flowers are blooming on the **Harriet Maxwell Wildflower Trail**. If so, it's definitely worth a visit. The seasonal **butterfly pavilion** is anther favorite for all ages. *Info:* 2101 N Galvin Parkway in Papago Park. Tel. 480-941-1225. www.dbg.org. Open daily October though April 8am-8pm; May-September 7am-8pm. Admission: $10 adults, $9 seniors, $4 children 3-12.

There are numerous places to hike within Metro Phoenix (see Phoenix Best Activities), but one of my favorites with visitors is the north central **Phoenix Mountain Preserve**. Most people come here to summit 2600 foot **Piestewa Peak** (formerly Squaw Peak.) Avoid the crowds by heading all the way to the end of the Squaw Peak Drive and hiking **Nature Trail #304** instead. You'll get the same experience of being surrounded by Sonoran Desert without bumping into all the people. You can hike for as little as half a mile, or put together a route that covers as many as ten miles. *Info:* Squaw Peak Drive near 24th Street and Glendale Ave. http://phoenix.gov/PARKS/hikephx.html. No admission fee.

After your hike, head a few miles south to lunch at the **Arizona Biltmore and Villas**. Influenced by the famous architect Frank Lloyd Wright, the Biltmore was one of the first luxury resorts in the valley. Notice as you approach the resort how the buildings harmonize with their natural surroundings. Take a walk around the grounds to admire the architectural details. Don't eat inside, but rather sit outside under the loggia at **The Café** (see *Phoenix Sleeps & Eats*). Relax as you look out over the manicured gardens to gaze at the mountains you just hiked.

Whether you hit the links, bike or rollerblade the **Indian Bend Wash Greenbelt**, or just lounge by your hotel pool, you can't go wrong with a little outdoor fun in the Valley of the Sun (see *Phoenix Best Activities*).

4. TUCSON

Located in a high desert valley surrounded by mountains, Tucson enjoys a climate somewhat cooler than that of Phoenix, but equally sunny. Older than Phoenix by a long shot, Tucson's Spanish-Colonial heritage is readily evident in the adobe and pueblo-style architecture that dominates the city.

Downtown is still the vibrant heart of Tucson and should not be missed. Just to the north of downtown is the University of Arizona with its multiple museums and well-regarded sports teams. There is great hiking in nearby Sabino Canyon and many other nearby spots, and beautiful outdoor attractions like Saguaro National Park and the Arizona-Sonora Desert Museum. Many excellent resorts are tucked into the mountains and foothills on the city's northern fringe.

ONE GREAT DAY IN TUCSON

With a day in Tucson you'll want to take in the city's signature highlights — both the wonderful Sonoran Desert and the historic *barrio* neighborhood downtown.

Grab a picnic lunch before you take off and then head west to the **Tucson Mountain Park,** covering 17,000 acres of mountains and desert. Enjoy the scenery along Gate Pass Road before turning right onto Kinney Road to visit the outstanding **Arizona-Sonora Desert Museum.** This wonderful facility is a place where nature comes to life and learning becomes fun for children and adults. Don't let the word "museum" fool you – it's really like a **zoo and botanical gardens** along with a natural history museum. You'll find more than 200 animals roaming in natural habitats, along with over 300 birds in walk-through aviaries. All of the animals and plants are native to the fascinating Sonoran Desert Environment. Don't miss the **Cave and Earth History Room** or the **Mountain Habitat** exhibit. You'll spend your entire morning here and be glad that you did. *Info:* 2021 North Kinney Road. Tel. 580-883-2702. www.desertmuseum.org. Open 8:30am-5:30pm daily (7:30am in summer). Saturdays in summer open until 10pm. $12 adults. $4 children 6-12. (Discounted rates in summer.)

Note: If you visit the museum in January-April, make reservations to eat lunch at the museums' outstanding **Ocotillo Café.** Using farm-fresh ingredients, the chefs prepare **wonderful Arizona-Sonora regional cuisine.** Open for lunch only in the winter and dinner on Saturday nights in the summer. (Tel. 520-883-5705.)

Lunch on the Set!

If you've got school-age kids in tow, they might prefer lunch at the Old Tucson Studios, a western movie set and theme park located on Kinney Road on the way back into town. (Tel. 520-883-0100.)

After touring the museum you can sit under the ramadas behind the entrance and enjoy your lunch while **taking in the wonderful views** of the museum property as well as the Saguaro National Park beyond. The museum's **Ironwood Terrace Restaurant** offers a variety of grab-and-go food (pizza, burgers, hotdogs) if you didn't have time to pack a lunch.

After lunch, head back 13 miles northeast into downtown to tour the **Barrio Historico and the El Presidio Historic District**. Founded in 1775, Tucson's downtown area still retains much of its Spanish colonial flavor. With adobe buildings and Spanish street names, you'll feel a sense of the past as you walk the avenues.

Start on foot at the intersection of Broadway and Stone, the heart of downtown. Walk two blocks south on Stone to see the beautiful **St. Augustine Cathedral**, modeled after the Cathedral of Queretaro in Mexico. From there, return to your starting point and head west on Broadway to the **Sosa-Carrillo-Fremont House**. This Mexican adobe-style dwelling has been carefully restored to look as it did in 1880 when John Fremont was the Territorial Governor. *Info:* 151 South Granada Ave. Tel. 520-622-0956. Open Wednesday-Saturday 10am-4pm. $3 adults. $2 children 12-18.

Next, walk over to North Main Avenue and the **El Presidio Park Historic District**. This is where Tucson first began and there are five historic homes on the block as well as the **Tucson Museum of Art**. The homes, built between the mid-1850s to 1907, house collections of Western and Latin American art. The Tucson Museum of Art contains exhibits that span region's history from pre-Colombian to Western American art. *Info:* 140 North Main Avenue. Tel. 520-624-2333. www.tucsonarts.com. Open Tuesday-Saturday 10am-4pm. $8 adults. $3 children 13-18.

ALTERNATIVE PLAN: If you'd rather hike after lunch than tour the Barrio Historico, the western section of **Saguaro National Park** abuts the Arizona-Sonora Desert Museum. Take off on the King Canyon trail, in walking distance from the museum, to wander through an amazing profusion of these most unique cactus specimens.

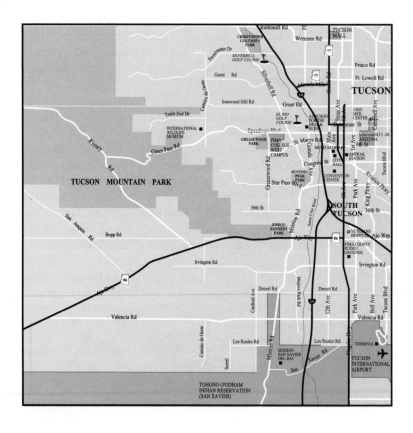

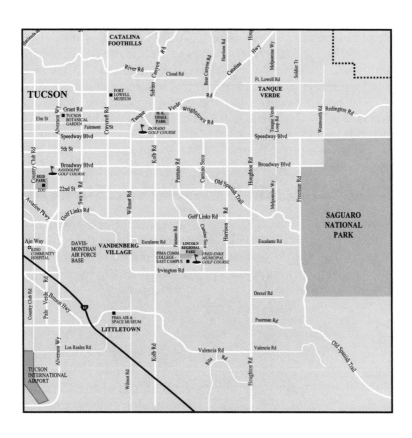

After a full day of touring you'll be ready for a cold margarita and excellent Mexican food at one of the two best Mexican restaurants in town. Both **Café Poca Cosa**, for high-end cuisine, and **El Charro**, for down-home Arizona-Mex flavors, deliver wonderful Mexican specialties. You can't go wrong with either one (see *Tucson Sleeps & Eats*).

After dinner, if you're still up for a night on the town, check out the **cutting edge music scene** at the **Club Congress** next to the Hotel Congress, on – you guessed it – Congress St. downtown (see *Tucson Nightlife*). Another option is to hit one of the **many bars** that line the University of Arizona's **4th Avenue**. This street, filled with shops and restaurants that cater to the University's student body, stays rocking late into the night. You can find everything from intimate wine bars to clubs jammed with dancing and drinking co-eds.

A FANTASTIC TUCSON WEEKEND

With a weekend in Tucson you can enjoy the best of what the city has to offer, from historic missions and museums to great shopping and restaurants; your food choices will range from fine dining in plush resorts to Indian fry bread sold out of a trailer. Don't forget the great outdoors, whether you are hiking through Giant Saguaros or just lounging poolside.

Friday Evening
Upon arrival, make your way to the **foothills of the Catalina**

Mountains to the Westin La Paloma (see *Tucson Sleeps & Eats*). This Spanish mission style resort is built into the side of the hill and the grounds are gorgeous. Head straight to the **mesquite shaded patio of the J-Bar** where you can watch the city lights twinkling below as darkness falls. Enjoy a refreshing drink and unwind from your week.

If you're up for a splurge, head to dinner at **Janos**, also on the hotel grounds. An extraordinary dining experience awaits you in this **historic adobe pueblo** constructed in the 1850s. Take your time savoring the **French-inspired southwestern cuisine** and extensive wine list.

Saturday
Start your morning at the **Cup Café** in the **historic Hotel Congress** downtown. Serving up everything from southwest-inspired omelets to vegan French toast, the Cup breakfast is a hip way to start your day (see *Tucson Sleeps & Eats*).

ALTERNATIVE PLAN: If you're on a budget, the J-Bar is an excellent spot for dinner as well (see previous page). The Latin American/Caribbean cuisine is grilled to perfection and both the atmosphere and price are a little more low-key than Janos.

Begin your walking tour of both the **Barrio Historico** (historic neighborhood) and **the El Presidio Historic District**. Founded in 1775, Tucson's downtown area, with adobe buildings and Spanish street names, still retains much of its Spanish colonial flavor.

Start on foot at the intersection of Broadway and Stone, the heart of downtown. Walk two blocks south on Stone to see the beautiful **St. Augustine Cathedral**, modeled after the Cathedral of Queretaro in Mexico. The original plans for the church outlined a Gothic style structure with thin pointed spires, but the spires were left unfinished for over 30 years because of lacking funds. Finally in 1928 the building was updated with a **Mexican baroque** look – including towers instead of spires.

Return to your starting point and head west on Broadway to the **Sosa-Carrillo-Fremont House**. This historic Mexican adobe-style dwelling has been carefully **restored to look as it did in 1880** when John Fremont was the Territorial Governor. There is also an exhibit about Tucson's Hispanic pioneer families. *Info:* 151 South Granada Ave. Tel. 520-622-0956. Open Wednesday-Saturday 10am-4pm. $3 adults. $2 children 12-18.

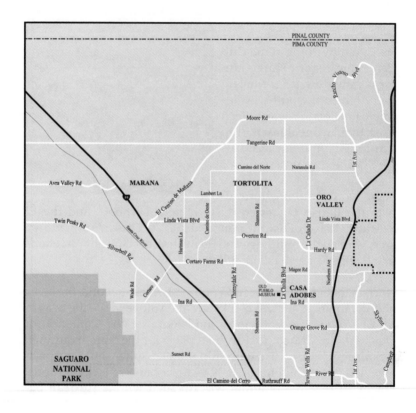

PINAL COUNTY
PIMA COUNTY

Rancho Vistoso Blvd

Moore Rd

Tangerine Rd

Camino del Norte   Naranula Rd

1st Ave

Avra Valley Rd   **MARANA**   **TORTOLITA**

El Camino de Mañana   Lambert Ln   **ORO VALLEY**

Twin Peaks Rd   Linda Vista Blvd   Camino de Oeste   Shannon Rd   La Cañada Dr   Linda Vista Blvd

Santa Cruz River   Hartman Ln   Overton Rd

Silverbell Rd   Hardy Rd

Cortaro Farms Rd   Magee Rd   Northern Ave

Wade Rd   Camino Rd   Thornydale Rd   OLD PUEBLO MUSEUM   La Cholla Blvd   **CASA ADOBES**   Skyline

Ina Rd   Ina Rd

Shannon Rd   Orange Grove Rd

Sunset Rd   La Cholla Blvd   Towing Wells Rd

SAGUARO NATIONAL PARK   El Camino del Cerro   Ruthrauff Rd   River Rd   1st Ave   Campbell

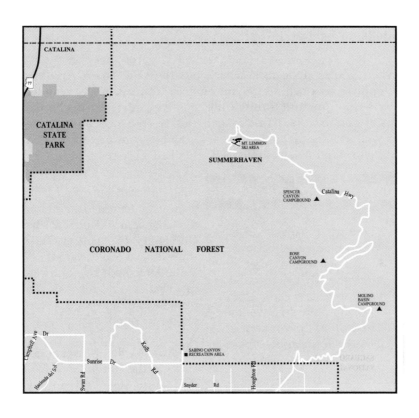

Continue your tour by walking over to North Main Avenue and the **El Presidio Park Historic District**. This center for the arts is where Tucson first began and there are **five historic homes** on the block as well as the **Tucson Museum of Art**. The homes, built between the mid-1850s to 1907, house collections of Western and Latin American art. The Tucson Museum of Art contains exhibits that span region's history from **pre-Colombian to Western American** art. *Info:* 140 North Main Avenue. Tel. 520-624-2333. www.tucsonarts.com. Open Tuesday-Saturday 10am-4pm. $8 adults. $3 children 13-18.

When you're done here, check out the **Old Town Artisans shopping area** behind the museum on Court Avenue. Wander from store to store through the massive courtyard inside the historic adobe. You'll find art galleries, Latin American imports, as well as handmade fine jewelry. The pleasant patio is a good place to stop for refreshments if you need a break.

Downtown Mexican Eats

There are so many excellent Mexican restaurants downtown that it would be hard to go wrong. My two favorites, however, are Café Poca Cosa, for more high-end flavors of Mexico, and El Charro, for classic, home-style AZ-Mex cuisine (see *Tucson Sleeps & Eats*).

After lunch head down University Boulevard to the attractive 320-acre campus of the **University of Arizona**. Take some time to walk around. Relax under a shady tree, and you can visit several museums, a planetarium, and an interesting center of photography.

The **Arizona State Museum**, devoted to the cultural development of the state, is **definitely worth a visit**. The collection of Hohokam and Mogollon culture artifacts is outstanding and some of the relics date back over 10,000 years. Scholars from all over the world come here to research the Southwest. *Info:* 1013 E. University Boulevard. Tel. 520-621-6302. www.statemuseum.arizona.edu. Open 10am-5pm Monday-Saturday, 12pm-5pm Sunday. Admission is free but a $3 donation is suggested.

The **Center for Creative Photography** also merits a stop. The collection includes more than 50,000 still pictures taken by photographers from all over the world, including big names like **Ansel Adams** and Edward Westin. *Info:* 1030 North Olive Road. Tel. 520-621-7968. www.creativephotography.org. Open 9am-5pm Monday-Friday, 12pm-5pm, Saturday-Sunday. Admission is free but a $5 donation is suggested.

Be sure to wander down **4ᵗʰ Avenue**, right off campus, to experience the **eclectic mix of shops and galleries** frequented by students. If you don't feel like walking the nine blocks of the shopping district you can take the **Old Pueblo Trolley**, which runs down the street.

For dinner, you can either hit one of the informal but **delicious ethnic eateries along 4ᵗʰ Avenue**, or enjoy the elegant restaurant at the nearby **Arizona Inn** (see *Tucson Sleeps & Eats*). After dinner, if you've still got it in you, head to one of the bars that line 4ᵗʰ Avenue, or make a complete circle of your day and end up at the **Club Congress**, next to the Congress Hotel, for **cutting edge rock music**.

> **ALTERNATIVE PLAN:** If you're in town in the summer months and want to get outdoors, **Mt. Lemmon**, at over 9,000 feet, is an excellent choice. Take the ski lift up and then hike one of the many trails that lead off from the top of the lift. During the cooler months you can hike pretty **Sabino Canyon** with its refreshing flowing creek (see *A Wonderful Week in Tucson* below.)

Sunday

Sunday is an appropriate day to get out and visit **Mission San Xavier del Bac**, on the Tohono O'odham Indian Reservation about fifteen miles from downtown. Dating from 1692, it remains active today. The current

mission, completed in 1797, is considered to be perhaps the **finest example of Spanish mission architecture ever built**. San Xavier should be seen even if you have no interest in churches. Climb the small hill to the east of the mission for a nice view of the property. Don't miss the chance to eat authentic Indian fry bread here as well. *Info:* Exit 92 off of I-19. Tel. 520-294-2624. Open 9:30am-5:30pm daily. No admission but donations requested.

Chile Relleno Heaven!

Stop by Mi Nidito in south Tucson for dinner on your way back into town. Kurt Russell, Willie Nelson, and former President Bill Clinton have all given this popular Mexican eatery the thumbs up. In fact, they named a rather hefty plate after Clinton. The chile rellenos are excellent. 1814 S. 4th Ave near intersection with 29th St. Tel. 520-622-5081.

On your way back into town, head 24 miles north to visit the wonderful **Arizona-Sonora Desert Museum**. Don't let the word "museum" fool you – it's really like a **zoo and botanical gardens** along with a natural history museum. You learn so much here without even trying. You'll find more than 200 animals roaming in natural habitats, along with over 300 birds in walk-through aviaries. All of the animals and plants are native to the Sonoran Desert. The **Woodland Mountain Habitat** trail is home to an impressive **mountain lion and even a black bear**. You'll definitely want to pause at the **prairie dog village** in the **Desert Grassland** section as well. *Info:* 2021 North Kinney Road. Tel. 580-883-2702. www.desertmuseum.org. Open 8:30am-5:30pm daily (7:30am in summer). Saturdays in summer open until 10pm. $12 adults. $4 children 6-12. (Discounted rates in summer.)

Spend your last hours hiking through the giant cactuses of nearby **Saguaro National Park** – the King Canyon Trail is in walking distance from the parking lot of the Desert Museum – or just **lounging poolside** enjoying the wonderful Tucson climate.

ALTERNATIVE PLAN: If you've been to Tucson before and want to explore **your inner cowpoke** for a weekend, nothing beats a stay at one of the nearby guest ranches. **White Stallion Ranch,** close to town but in a world of its own, is one of the best bets in the state for a wonderful dude ranch experience (see *Tucson Sleeps & Eats*).

A WONDERFUL WEEK IN TUCSON

With a week in Tucson you can see all the best sights in town, spend some time in the great outdoors, and take a few interesting day trips as well.

RECOMMENDED PLAN: Spend two days exploring the historic district downtown and the University of Arizona. Spend another day on the west side of town learning about the Sonoran Desert, hiking among Giant Saguaros, and visiting the wonderful San Xavier del Bac. The east side of town with its section of the Saguaro National Park and Sabino Canyon merits a day as well. Spend another three days road tripping to Mexico and visiting historic western and mining towns south and east of Tucson.

Historic Downtown

Tucson proper was founded in 1775 when a Spanish presidio, or fortified post, was established on the banks of the Santa Cruz River. While few of the original structures remain, Tucson's downtown area, with adobe buildings and Spanish street names, still retains much of its Spanish colonial flavor. Experience this *sabor latino* with a walking tour of both the **Barrio Historico** (historic neighborhood) and **the El Presidio Historic District**.

Start at the intersection of Broadway and Stone, the heart of downtown. Walk two blocks

Don't Miss...

• Historic downtown – barrio, art district
• Arizona-Sonora Desert Museum – gorgeous flora and fauna
• San Xavier del Bac – classic Spanish mission, great architecture
• Saguaro National Park – like a parade of giant cacti
• Bisbee – fun Old West mining town
• Chiricahua National Monument – unique, breathtaking rock formations

south on Stone to see the beautiful **St. Augustine Cathedral**, modeled after the Cathedral of Queretaro in Mexico. The original plans for the church outlined a Gothic style structure with thin pointed spires, but the spires were left unfinished for over 30 years because of lacking funds. Finally in 1928 the building was updated with a **Mexican baroque** look – including towers instead of spires.

> ## Start the Day at the Cup Cafe
>
> Fortify yourself before you begin with breakfast at the wonderful Cup Café in the historic Hotel Congress downtown. It's also a great spot for lunch and dinner featuring an Asian/Latin flair (see *Tucson Sleeps & Eats*).

Return to your starting point and head west on Broadway to the **Sosa-Carrillo-Fremont House**. This historic Mexican adobe-style dwelling has been carefully **restored to look as it did in 1880** when John Fremont was the Territorial Governor. There is also an exhibit about Tucson's Hispanic pioneer families. *Info:* 151 South Granada Ave. Tel. 520-622-0956. Open Wednesday-Saturday 10am-4pm. $3 adults. $2 children 12-18.

Continue your tour by walking over to North Main Avenue and the **El Presidio Park Historic District**. This center for the arts is where Tucson first began and there are **five historic homes** on the block as well as the **Tucson Museum of Art**. The homes, built between the mid-1850s to 1907, house collections of Western and Latin American art. The Tucson Museum of Art contains exhibits that span region's history from **pre-Colombian to Western American** art. It also has a great gift shop and cafe. *Info:* 140 North Main Avenue. Tel. 520-624-2333. www.tucsonarts.com. Open Tuesday-Saturday 10am-4pm. $8 adults. $3 children 13-18.

If shopping is your thing, don't miss the **Old Town Artisans shopping area** behind the museum on Court Avenue. The **historic adobe** houses a number of stores around its courtyard, such as art galleries, Latin American import shops, as well as jewelers. The pleasant patio is a good place to stop for refreshments if you need a break.

And if there are kids in your group, you might want to check out the nearby **Tucson Children's Museum**. The museum promotes understanding and interest in science and history through **interactive displays**. There's also a Dinosaur Canyon and **Sonoran Sea Aquarium**. *Info:* 1200 S. 6th Ave. Tel. 520-792-9985. www.tucsonchildrensmuseum.org. Open Tuesday-Saturday 10am-5pm. Sunday 12pm-5pm. $5.50 adults, $3.50 children 2-16.

University of Arizona

The attractive 320-acre university campus is part of what makes Tucson such a vibrant city. In addition to walking around campus and relaxing under a shady tree, you should visit some of the attractions that include a number of museums, a planetarium, and a center for photography. The campus itself is a **botanical garden of sorts** featuring desert plants from all over the world. Check the local paper before you head down to the university so that you can time your visit to catch any campus sporting or cultural events that might peak your interest.

Your fist stop should be the **Arizona State Museum**, devoted to the cultural development of the state. The collection of Hohokam and Mogollon culture artifacts is the best in the world and some of the relics date back over 10,000 years. Scholars from all over come here to research the Southwest. The well-marked exhibits are arranged in chronological order. A huge display **explains the cultures of many of Arizona's native groups**, including the locally important Tohono O'odhams. *Info:* 1013 E. University Boulevard. Tel. 520-621-6302. www.statemuseum.arizona.edu. Open 10am-5pm Monday-Saturday, 12pm-5pm Sunday. Admission is free but a $3 donation is suggested.

The 4th Avenue Scene

Be sure to wander down 4th Avenue, right off campus, to experience the eclectic mix of shops, galleries, ethnic restaurants, and bars frequented by students. If you don't feel like walking the nine blocks of the shopping district you can take the Old Pueblo Trolley, which runs down the street.

The **Center for Creative Photography** also merits a stop. The collection includes more than 50,000 still pictures taken by photographers from all over the world. In fact, it houses the entire collections of **Ansel Adams,** Edward Westin, and other important artists. *Info:* 1030 North Olive Rd. Tel. 520-621-7968. www.creativephotography.org. Open 9am-5pm Monday-Friday, 12pm-5pm, Saturday-Sunday. Admission is free but a $5 donation is suggested.

Stargazers of all ages will appreciate the newly designed **Flandreau Science Center and Planetarium**. With the goal of being a living and working laboratory designed to offer the ultimate in sensory exploration, the center has a set of **prototype exhibits and planetarium programs** for the public to experience and evaluate. *Info:* 1601 E. University Blvd. Tel. 520-621-7827. www.flandreau.org. Check website or call for hours and admission prices.

West Tucson
Tucson's wonderful **Arizona-Sonora Desert Museum** is a must on any visitor's list. Don't let the word "museum" fool you – it's

really like **a zoo and botanical gardens** along with a natural history museum. Almost two-miles of pathways lead through exhibits of the various ecological zones of the Sonoran Desert. You'll find more than 200 animals roaming in natural habitats, along with over 300 birds in walk-through aviaries. Some of my favorite sections are the **Woodland Mountain Habitat** trail, with its impressive **mountain lion**, as well as the **hummingbird aviary**. You'll definitely want to pause at the **prairie dog village** in the Desert **Grassland** section as well. *Info:* 2021 North Kinney Road. Tel. 580-883-2702. www.desertmuseum.org. Open 8:30am-5:30pm daily (7:30am in summer). Saturdays in summer open until 10pm. $12 adults. $4 children 6-12. (Discounted rates in summer.)

Adjacent to the museum is the western section of the **outstanding Saguaro National Park**. In fact, the King Canyon Trail is in walking distance from the museum's parking lot. This section of the park hosts a diverse display of natural flora because of the variation in altitudes, but the highlight is the park's namesake, the **Giant Saguaro Cactus**. The **Red Hills Visitor Center** explains the saguaro ecosystem in detail. Even if you don't want to hike, you should definitely **drive along Kinney Road**, which winds through the park and its almost mind-boggling number of saguaros. It is literally like a forest in some places. *Info:* West Tucson: Tucson Mountain District. Tel. 520-733-5153. www.nps.gov/sagu. Open daily 7am-sunset. Visitor Center 9am-5pm. $10 per car.

Called the "White Dove of the Desert," **Mission San Xavier del Bac**, on the Tohono O'odham Indian Reservation southwest of town, is a Tucson highlight. The mission was founded in the late 1600s and is still active today. The current church, completed in 1797, is considered to be perhaps the **finest example of Spanish mission architecture** ever built. Of greatest interest are the many domes, elaborate carvings and extensive use of **flying buttresses**. The interior is gorgeous as well.

Old West Movie Set

School-age kids might like to visit the Old Tucson Studios, a western movie set and theme park located on Kinney Road near the Arizona-Sonora Desert Museum. A functioning movie set for westerns, it also features train rides, a carousel, and a daily gunfight. The price, to me, is a little steep for what you get, but many families and foreign tourists seem to enjoy it. (Tel. 520-883-0100. www.oldtucson.com)

San Xavier is worth a visit even if you have no interest in churches. Climb the small hill to the east of the mission for a nice overview of the property. And if fried food is alright with you, then indulge in some delicious, **authentic Indian fry bread** here. *Info:* Exit 92 off of I-19. Tel. 520-294-2624. Open 9:30am-5:30pm daily. No admission charge but donations are requested.

East Tucson
Sabino Canyon, a true oasis, is one of the highlights of the east side

of town. Stop by the visitor center to see exhibits on the flora and fauna of this part of the higher Sonoran Desert before riding the tram four miles into the narrow canyon. There are stops along the way so you can get out and **soak your feet in the refreshing pools** of the creek. Even better, get out and hike some of the many miles of trails. *Info:* Off of Tanque Verde Rd: end Sabino Canyon Road. Tel. 520-749-2861. www.sabinocanyon.com. Open 9am-4:30pm daily with tram rides every hour on the hour. $7.50 adults. $3 children 3-12.

Our Kind of Pit Stop

The wonderful **Montana Avenue restaurant** is a convenient and delicious stop on the way back from the canyon. Featuring **updated twists on southwestern cuisine**, the restaurant has a lovely patio as well as a sleek, contemporary interior (see *Tucson Sleeps & Eats*).

Very near Sabino Canyon is the interesting **DeGrazia Gallery in the Sun**. Set amid the pretty Santa Catalina Mountains, the gallery displays the paintings and sculpture of **artist Ted DeGrazia**. I find his paintings a little hokey, but some people love them and the setting is nice. Perhaps of greater interest is the adjacent **beautiful open-air chapel** that he built and decorated extensively with frescos. *Info:* Five miles east of downtown off of Broadway: 6300 N Swan Drive. Tel. 520-299-9192. www.degrazia.org. Open 7am-3:45pm daily. Admission free.

Another great opportunity to enjoy the Sonoran Desert can be found in the **Rincon Mountain District** of **Saguaro National Park**. The main draw here is the **spectacular paved Cactus Forest Drive**. This is the real heart of the Saguaro Forest, where hundreds of the tallest saguaros can easily be seen from the road. Many long trails that rise to the higher elevations of Rincon Mountain are available for hiking. *Info:* East Tucson: Rincon Mountain District off

of Broadway. Tel. 520-733-5153. www.nps.gov/sagu. Open daily 7am-sunset. Visitor Center 9am-5pm. $10 per car.

Gardens

If you're a fan of botanical gardens, there are two excellent options I highly recommend. **Tohono Chul Botanical Park**, a lovely 50-acre site on the north side of town, educates the public about the historic, cultural, and environmental values of the Southwest desert regions. **Stroll the tranquil trails** or browse the small gallery. The park also has a **lovely restaurant** where you can get a great lunch. *Info:* North of downtown: 7366 Paseo del Norte. Tel. 520-575-8468. www.tucsonmuseums.org. Open 8am-5pm daily. $5 adults. $2 children 5-12.

The **Tucson Botanical Gardens** are also quite nice. Smaller and closer to downtown, the five-acre property features a **collection of 16 specialty gardens**. Especially nice are the Backyard Bird and Butterfly gardens. *Info:* Northeast of downtown: 2150 N. Alvernon Way. Tel 520-326-9686. www.tucsonbotanical.org. Open 8:30am-4:30pm daily. $5 adults. $2.50 children 6-12.

Remember **Biosphere 2**, the enclosed ecosystem designed to test the recycling capabilities of air, water, and nutrients? The experiment didn't work very well, but it was a cool concept. It's still an interesting place to visit. You too can **survive inside the 3-acre structure** on a guided tour. The tour includes visits to the tropical savanna, the million gallon tropical ocean, and the geodesic domes that kept the whole thing from imploding. *Info:* Thirty miles north of Tucson on AZ-77. Tel. 520-838-6200. www.bio2.com.

Take Flight!

Aviation buffs and even those just fascinated by big things will enjoy the Pima Air and Space Museum. The entire history of aviation in America can be traced through the museum's collection of over 200 vintage aircraft that are located along pathways and in hangers. There's even a former Air Force One. *Info:* Exit 95 (Valencia Rd) off of I-19: 6000 East Valencia Road. Tel. 520-574-9658. www.pimaair.org. Open 9am-5pm daily. $11.75 adults. $6 children 7-12 (slightly cheaper in summer.)

Day Trips South of Tucson

The region south of Tucson features a **wonderful variety** of places to see, from frontier and border towns, to caves and crazy stone formations. I've outlined four trips below. You could also combine a few of them, spending the night in one of the cities mentioned.

Nogales, Mexico

This adventure, which includes a visit across the border to Mexico, covers about 200 miles, almost all of which is on Interstate 19. The total drive time there and back will only take a little over three hours, giving you plenty of time to visit the sites and do some shopping on Old Mexico.

About 30 miles south of Tucson take exit 69 to Green Valley and follow the signs to the **Titan Missile Museum**. This unique facility is a **former ICBM launch site**. At one time there were more than 50 of these scattered across the US, but happily this is the only one that remains. It looks just like it did in its operational days, including the missile in its silo – warhead removed of course. Fascinating one-hour guided tours lead you down several flights of stairs to the control center and include a **simulated launch sequence**. Whatever your politics, nuclear weaponry is an important part of our nation's history. *Info:* Exit 69 off I-19. Tel. 520-625-7736. www.pimaair.org. Open 9am-5pm daily. $8.50 adults. $5 children 7-12.

Continue south on I-19 to Exit 34 and the small town of **Tubac**. Tubac dates prior to the arrival of the Spaniards and amazingly, was the most populous town in Arizona at one point in the middle of the 19th century. Today it is primarily an artist's community. You can stop by both the **Tubac Presidio State Historic Park** (Tel. 520-398-2252), with a display of part of the original fort, as well as the **Tumacacori National Historic Park** (Tel. 520-398-2341), which preserves a **huge Franciscan church** that was started in 1800 but never finished. Both are open daily from 8am-5pm.

Traveling another 20 miles south will take you to the border town of Nogales, Arizona, which is located directly across from its

Mexican sister city, **Nogales, Mexico.** While there isn't much to see on either side of the border, many people like to cross over to say they went to another country on their vacation. Take advantage of the **busy and colorful markets** right across on the Mexican side where you can get some **excellent values on high-quality artisania** including clothing, pottery and jewelry. (To

Nogales's Best Eats

Enjoy a meal at one of the popular restaurants on the Mexican side of the border. Try La Roca, Calle Elias 91, or El Greco, on the corner of Obregon and Pierson, for wonderful food and outstanding service.

get to the markets, turn right on Campillo Street and walk down three blocks to Obregon.) Don't drive over, rather park your car in one of the guarded lots on the US side and walk across. It's best to be back across by dark. Due to post-9/11 security concerns, you now officially need to have a passport to get back in the US.

Kartchner Caverns/Sonoita/Patagonia Loop
This trip takes you underground to a fascinating cave, as well as to the Arizona Wine Country and a revitalized old western town.

Take I-10 south to exit 302 and the town of Benson. From there follow the signs to AZ-90 and nine miles later you'll reach **Kartchner Caverns State Park.** The newest member of the Arizona State Parks, this large system of **beautiful limestone caves** was first discovered in 1974, but kept secret for 14 years. All of this time was used to prepare the caverns to minimize visitor impact on the delicate and pristine environment. Take an hour-long guided tour, whose highlights include **two rooms that are more than a hundred feet high and longer than a football field**, as well as the Kubla Kahn cave column and a 17-foot soda straw. All of the cave walks are well lit, paved and not overly strenuous. If you only visit one cave in Arizona, this should be it, although the entry fee is quite pricey. *Info:* AZ 90 south of Benson. Tel. 520-586-2283. www.azstateparks.com. Open 7:30am-6pm daily. $5 per car in addition to tour fees. Tours - $23 adults. $13 children 7-13. Reservations recommended.

Continue south on AZ-90 to the intersection with AZ-82 and head west towards the **vineyards and wineries of Sonoita**. Although Arizona and quality wine might sound like an oxymoron, there are actually some good wines being produced by **Callaghan Vineyards** (www.callaghanvineyards.com, Tel. 520-455-5322) and decent ones by **Sonoita Vineyards** (www.sonoitavineyards.com, Tel. 455-5893) Callaghan's Back Lot Cuvee is known as the best of the region. Regardless of the quality of the wine, the **grasslands scenery is so nice** that you might want to stay a while.

Sonoita, in fact, has several good restaurants and inns. The town is an easy, romantic get-away spot for Tucsonans. Try **Café Sonoita** (3280 AZ-82, Tel. 520-455-5278) for a culinary treat, and **La Hacienda de Sonoita** (34 Swanson Road, Tel. 455-5308,) for a cozy B&B if you decide to spend the night.

Head south down AZ-82 for another 12 miles to reach the little mountain town of **Patagonia**. Known both as an **artists' hamlet** and an **international birding ground**, Patagonia has attracted a unique type of citizen. Located at 4,000 feet, the town stays decently cool in the summer, so you can visit year-round. Wander the streets of town visiting the **galleries and shops**, or head to the two areas famous for their diversity of birdlife. Even if you're not a birder, the **Nature Conservancy's Patagonia-Sonoita Creek Preserve** (150 Blue Heaven Road, Tel. 520-394-2400, open Wednesday–Sunday, 7:30am-4pm) and the **Patagonia Lake State Park** (400 Patagonia Lake Road, Tel. 520-287-6965, open 8am-10pm) are both pleasant areas for hiking and picnics.

Patagonia's Hub!

To get a real sense of Patagonia, all you have to do is hang out at the **Gathering Grounds Coffee Shop** (319 McKeown Avenue, Tel. 520-394-2097) for a while. This coffee, breakfast and sandwich shop even serves dinner and has live music on weekend nights.

Tombstone & Bisbee

This little trip is all about the Old West. Take 1-10 to exit 303 in Benson and pick up AZ-80 for 24 miles to the historic town of **Tombstone**. One of Arizona's most popular tourist destinations, it is filled with history and is especially fun for kids. It **appears much the same as it did in the 1880s** when it was one of the most infamous of the Wild West's mining communities. Don't miss **Boot Hill**, the final resting place of a few  notorious criminals, the **Crystal Palace Saloon**, where you can still knock back a whiskey, or the **Bird Cage Theater** (aka brothel), which had the reputation for being one of the the wildest establishments in the west. Also in town is the **OK Corral**, the location of America's most famous western gunfight between the **Earp Brothers** and the Clanton gang. The shoot-out is reenacted daily at 2pm.

Historic Fare in Tombstone

In Tombstone, drop by the Lamplight Room (108 N. 4th St., Tel. 520-457-3716), part of a historic B&B, to enjoy a meal where the entrees are made from recipes found in a cookbook from the 1880s. They also have a Mexican food menu if you prefer that.

Leave Tombstone by continuing on AZ-80 for 24 more miles to **Bisbee**. With the discovery of the Copper Queen Lode during the 1880s, Bisbee became one of the largest towns between St. Louis and San Francisco. While Tombstone is almost entirely a historic tourist site, Bisbee combines a visit to the past with a thriving modern community. It is picturesquely located in the mountain shadows of Mule Pass and is a wonderful place to spend a few hours or even a few days. The **Bisbee Mining and Historical Museum** on Main Street is a good place to learn about the town's past, while the **Muheim Heritage House** on Youngblood offers a look at the digs of a wealthy Bisbee businessman from 1898. Don't miss the **Queen Mine** at the south end of town, where former miners conduct tours in an **old mining car that actually takes you into an underground copper mine**. Wear a couple of layers under your mining outfit because it's 47 degrees in there.

Bisbee may be tiny, but there's nothing small-town about the quality of the restaurants and inns here. The delightful **Café Roka** (35 Main St., Tel. 520-432-5153) is the only restaurant in rural Arizona to have received a 3-Diamond rating from AAA. For a place to rest your head, try the **Canyon Rose Suites** (27 Subway St., Tel. 866-296-7673,) for large historical rooms, or the **Copper Queen Hotel** (11 Howell Ave, Tel. 520-432-2216) for a room with ghosts!

Willcox & the Chiricahua National Monument

Take I-10 to Exit 340 and the town of Willcox, a commercial center for the many surrounding ranching operations. The town has a long history of struggles with the Apache Indians, including the famous Geronimo. Check out the Rex Allen Arizona Cowboy Museum (150 N. Railroad Ave, Tel. 520-384-4583) for all the history of Willcox's most famous native son.

The history of the Indian Wars is outlined at the **Fort Bowie National Historic Site**, about 30-miles outside of town. Established in 1862 to protect the Butterfield Stage Route from attacks by the Apache, the fort was an **isolated and dangerous outpost**. It's still pretty isolated today and all that's left are some crumbling walls. Signs along the trail outline other historical sites and moments. From Willcox drive southeast for 20 miles on AZ-186 to the Fort Bowie turn off, then drive another eight miles on the unpaved road to the Fort Bowie Trailhead. It's another mile and a half walk to the ruins from there. *Info:* Tel. 520-847-2500. www.nps.gov/fobo/index.htm. Open 8am-4:30pm daily. No admission charge.

Return to AZ-186 and continue south to **Chiricahua National Monument**, one of Arizona's most **beautiful but relatively unknown natural wonders**. Situated in the Chiricahua Mountains, the area is known as the **Wonderland of Rocks**. The mountains rise sharply from the surrounding arid lowlands and provide a haven for many types of wildlife.

Chiricahua's gray rocks often take unusual shapes and forms ranging from the sublime to the almost grotesque. Many of the park's best features can be seen from the **Scenic Drive**, an 8-mile long one-way trip to the crest of the mountain. Some of the most unusual formations include Organ Pipe Rocks, Sea Captain, and China Boy. **Massai Point** at the end of the road offers a **fabulous panorama of tree-covered mountains and huge rock formations**. There is wonderful hiking here as well, especially the Echo Canyon and Heart of Rocks trails. *Info:* AZ 186. Tel. 520-824-3560. www.nps.gov/chir. Open 8am-4:30pm daily. $5 adults. Children under 16 free.

Dining options are slim out here. Bring a picnic and enjoy it from one of the scenic overlooks in Chiricahua, or try the **Desert Rose Café** in Willcox (706 South Haskell Ave., Tel. 520-384-0514).

5. NORTH-CENTRAL ARIZONA

A **wonderland for recreational opportunities**, this region is located almost entirely within National Forests. **Flagstaff**, located at the northern end of the region, is both a gateway to the Grand Canyon and a wonderful high-alpine getaway. It features a lively downtown, miles of hiking and mountain biking, interesting national monuments, and the best snow skiing in the state. **Sedona**, about 30 miles south of Flagstaff, is tucked into some of the prettiest scenery in the country. Soaring red rocks, dotted with green juniper, rise and twist into unforgettable formations. You can explore these surreal formation on foot, by jeep, or on horseback and then return to a town laced with art galleries, restaurants, and fine hotels.

The back road route from Sedona winds through the pines up to the historic and picturesque mining town of **Jerome**, which is now primarily an artist colony. From there you can make your way to **Prescott**, a town whose cowboy heritage is very much alive and on display even today.

ONE GREAT DAY IN NORTH-CENTRAL ARIZONA

Visitors love North-Central Arizona because it is so different from the Phoenix desert yet is only a couple of hours away from the Valley. If you've only got a day, you'll want to experience both the stunning red-rock vistas of Sedona as well as the pine-covered mountains in Flagstaff. Add excellent meals and outdoor opportunities and you'll have the perfect day.

The mild year-round climate and surreal red rock formations draw people to Sedona. An **artist's colony** in the '50s and '60s, Sedona now also draws hoards of nature lovers, spiritual seekers, and vacationing tourists.

Start your morning in Sedona with breakfast at the lovely Four-Diamond **L'Auberge de Sedona** (see *Sedona Sleeps & Eats*). While dinner here would set you back a pretty penny, insiders know that the **resort's gourmet breakfast** costs about the same as a morning meal would at Denny's. Hidden along the creek bed in the center of town, L'Auberge is the perfect place to experience Sedona's "cosmic energy." Walk the grounds to admire **gurgling Oak Creek** as well as the **stunning red rock views** before you enter the restaurant.

The best way to experience the red rocks is to **immerse yourself in them** with a hike. After breakfast, head south on 179 towards the Village of Oak Creek to **Bell Rock**. You can simply walk out and climb around on the mesmerizing Bell Rock (easy option), or enjoy the mostly-level five-mile loop hike around stunning Bell Rock and Courthouse Buttes. Look for the appropriately named Spaceship Rock on the backside of the loop. Bell Rock is a vortex

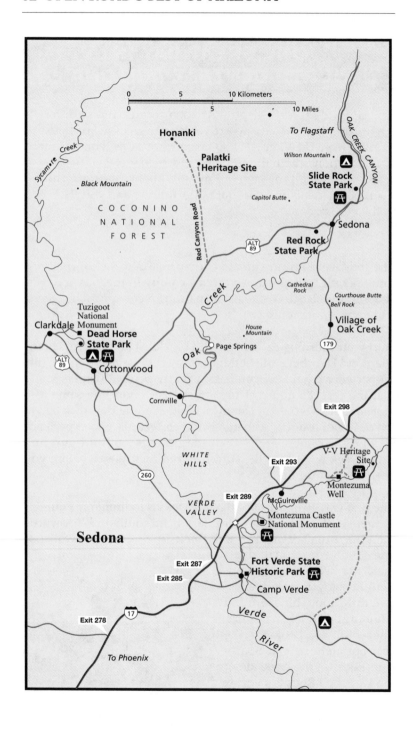

site. *Info*: 6.4 miles south of the 89/179 "Y" on 179. The trailhead and parking will be on your left. $5 Red Rock Pass required. You can buy passes at the trailhead or any of the Visitor's Centers.

After your hike, head back up 179 to visit the **Chapel of the Holy Cross**. Built into the area's native red rock and approached by a gently sloping ramp, the structure is **situated between two huge sandstone peaks**. Even if you don't have a religious bone in your body, you're sure to be moved by the **splendid panoramic view** from this locale. *Info*: Located on Chapel Road off of AZ 179 three miles south of the "Y." Tel. 928-282-4069. Open daily 9am-5pm. No admission fee but donations accepted.

Experience the Vortex!

You won't be in Sedona long before you read or hear about "**vortex sites**." The sites are apparently places where one can experience a concentration of swirling, uplifting energy. The twisted juniper trees found at many of the sites are offered as evidence of the strong energetic fields. You can take them with a grain of salt or seek them out, but either way, they're an integral part of Sedona.

If you like to shop, you can spend a while **walking through the stores of uptown** Sedona's Main Street before grabbing a **tasty Mexican lunch** at Oaxaca Restaurant (see Sedona Sleeps & Eats). If the weather is agreeable be sure to ask for patio seating with its awesome views.

After lunch you'll drive to Flagstaff on 89A via **scenic Oak Creek Canyon**. The road twists and turns from red rock spires up through pine and juniper trees to the edge of the Colorado Plateau. In many places the **sheer cliffs of the canyon** will tower a thousand feet or more about you. **Unusual rock formations and impressive deep gorges** complete the scene. Take the time to safely view the scenery from the many pullouts along the way, especially the **Oak Creek Vista** overlook at the top of the canyon. This is also the site of a **Native American crafts cooperative**.

Flagstaff is a wonderful mountain town that is about **25 degrees cooler than Phoenix** on average. People flock to Flag year-round, but summer is an especially popular time.

Once in Flagstaff, follow signs to Highway 180 and the **Museum of Northern Arizona**. The extremely well done museum explores the complete culture of the **Colorado Plateau region**. Choose whether you are most interested in anthropology, biology, geology, or the fine arts of the region and visit that section of the museum. Check out the lava bomb in the geology section. *Info:* Three miles north of town on Highway 180 (3101 North Fort Valley Road.) Tel. 928-774-5213. www.musnaz.org. Open daily 9am-5pm. Admission $5 adults; $2 children 7-17.

After visiting the museum head back on 180 to historic downtown Flagstaff. With a decidedly collegiate and mountain-town feel, Flagstaff is very different from the other cities in the state.

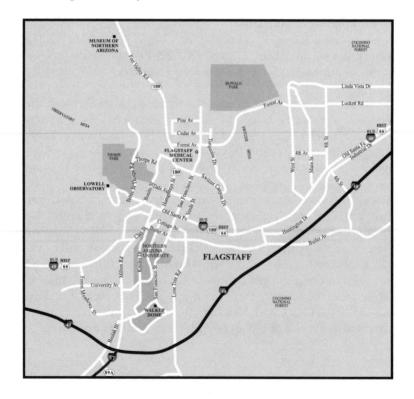

While downtown, you can wander through the many **unique shops and galleries** or just enjoy the scene at **Heritage Square**.

Stop in for a drink at downtown's **The Wine Loft**, a fun wine shop over an art gallery that serves wonderful wines by the glass (see *Flagstaff Nightlife*). They encourage you to linger by providing board games, tasting options, and nice art.

After your drink, walk south across the train tracks (watch

ALTERNATIVE PLAN: If hiking isn't your thing, you should use your time in Sedona to drive the **Red Rock Loop** west of town on 89A for spectacular views. You'll see the lovely formations of **Red Rock State Park** as well as the magnificent hoodoos and spires of **Cathedral Rock**. *Info*: The paved Red Rock Loop Road is located west of Sedona off of 89A. If you wish to enter Red Rock State Park there is a $5 entry fee.

out for the over 80 trains a day that come barreling through) to the **Beaver Street Brewery**, where you can enjoy awesome burgers, sandwiches, pizza, and micro-brewed beer. If it's nice outside ask for seating in the beer garden (see *Flagstaff Sleeps & Eats*). Once you're done with dinner, check out a show at the historic downtown **Orpheum Theater**. Constructed in 1917 as the town's movie house, it now showcases national touring acts (see *Flagstaff Nightlife*).

If you want to enjoy gourmet Flagstaff instead of a brew pub, don't miss the fantastic **Josephine's Modern American Bistro** located in a historic craftsman-style home (see *Flagstaff Sleeps & Eats*).

A FANTASTIC WEEK IN NORTH-CENTRAL ARIZONA

A weekend in the region will give you plenty of time to experience the dramatic red rock landscapes of Sedona as well as enjoy the mountain-town vibe and pine-covered hills of Flagstaff. You won't believe you're only two hours from Phoenix as you hike, drive and explore the best of the area.

Friday Evening
You'll start your weekend in Flagstaff, but if you're driving in from Phoenix in the afternoon you should make a stop at the impressive **Montezuma Castle National Monument** on your way up. This cliff dwelling is an excellent example of Sinagua architecture. Built into the hollow of a vertical cliff, the **five-story dwelling** was constructed in the early part of the 12th century. It's well worth a visit. *Info*: Exit 289, three miles off Interstate 17. Tel. 928-567-3322. www.nps.gov/moca/index.htm. Open daily 8am-5pm (6pm in summer). Admission $5 ages 16 and over.

Hit **downtown Flagstaff** in the evening. Browse the **shops and galleries** or just sit on a bench in **Heritage Square** to watch hacky-sackers, bongo drummers, and other college-town characters. Try the **Wine Loft**, an upstairs wine bar and gallery, for a relaxed yet sophisticated happy hour ambiance (see *Flagstaff Nightlife*).

There are a surprising number of high quality dining options in Flagstaff. If you want a comfortable, mountain-town atmosphere, try the **Beaver Street Brewery** for micro-brews and burgers. If you want fantastic high-end cuisine, both the **Cottage Place** and **Josephine's Modern American Bistro** are Wine Spectator Award of Excellence winners (see *Flagstaff Sleeps & Eats*).

ALTERNATIVE PLAN: If you'd rather **stargaze** than boot-scoot, consider an evening tour at the **Lowell Observatory**. Depending on the time of year, you may see the moon, planets, or globular and open star clusters through their 24-inch Clark Telescope. *Info*: 1400 West Mars Hill Road. Tel. 928-774-3358. www.lowell.edu. Open for both day and evening tours. Extended summer hours. Admission $5 adults. $2 children 5-17.

After dinner, swing by the historic **Museum Club** on **Route 66** (see *Flagstaff Nightlife*). A classic **roadhouse**, the Museum Club features live entertainment on weekends. Dance the night away under the neon signs.

Saturday
If you're in the mood for a hearty sit-down breakfast, don't miss the great chow at **Bellavista** on Beaver Street. If you'd rather grab and go, **Macy's**, next door to Bellavista, is a fantastic local coffee shop (see *Flagstaff Sleeps & Eats*).

After breakfast, head out Highway 180 to the wonderful **Museum of Northern Arizona**. Exploring the **culture of the Colorado Plateau** through the anthropology, biology, geology, and fine arts of the region, the museum offers something for everyone. Kids will like the replica dinosaur in the geology section. There are also nature trails and a pond for visitors to enjoy. *Info*: Three miles north of town on Highway 180 (3101 North Fort Valley Road.) Tel. 928-774-5213. www.musnaz.org. Open daily 9am-5pm. Admission $5 adults; $2 children 7-17.

If you went fancy for dinner last night, now's the time to try the **Beaver Street Brewery** for lunch. If you ate at the Brewery last night, **Salsa Brava** is a good bet for *delicioso* Mexican cuisine.

After lunch you'll head to Sedona via 89A through the impressive and scenic **Oak Creek Canyon**. You'll start in an environment of pine and juniper trees and then twist and turn down to Sedona's red rock spires.

In many places the **sheer cliffs of the canyon** will tower a thousand feet or more about you. Don't miss the **Oak Creek Vista** overlook as you start your descent. You'll get great view of the canyon as well as have the opportunity to buy Native American items at the **crafts cooperative**.

If you want to stretch your legs, stop on the way down (17.5 miles south of Flagstaff) at the **West Fork Hiking Trail**. One of the most popular hikes in the region, the trail meanders along, over, and through the creek sheltered by soaring red rock cliffs. (Wear shoes you don't mind getting wet.)

After your hike you'll be hungry for dinner. Try **Reds Bistro** at the Sedona Rouge Hotel. Contemporary yet comfortable, the eclectic menu will make everybody happy. Even the quesadillas on the kid's menu are gourmet (see *Sedona Sleeps & Eats*).

ALTERNATIVE PLAN: If you want to experience the Colorado Plateau first hand, drive up to Flagstaff's **Arizona Snowbowl**. During the summer the resort's chair lift is used to carry visitors up the mountain to 11,500 feet. From the top there are **spectacular views** of northern Arizona. (and delightfully cool temperatures.) There are also excellent **hikes** that start near the base of the chair lift and a **disc golf course**. During the winter you can enjoy **skiing and snowboarding** from the same spot. *Info:* Take Highway 180 seven miles north of Flagstaff to Snowbowl Road and continue up the mountain seven miles. Tel. 928-779-1951. www.arizonasnowbowl.com. Costs and hours vary depending on activity.

Sunday

Today's the day to get out and enjoy the inspiring red rocks of Sedona. Fuel yourself before you go with breakfast at the wonderful Four-Diamond **L'Auberge de Sedona** (see Sedona Sleeps & Eats). Insiders know that the **resort's gourmet breakfast** costs about the same as a morning meal would at a diner. Hidden besides gurgling Oak Creek in the center of town, L'Auberge is a wonderful place to savor Sedona's "cosmic energy."

The best way to experience Sedona is to spend some **time on the rocks**. After breakfast, head south on 179 towards the Village of Oak Creek to **Bell Rock**. You can simply walk out to Bell Rock (easy option), or enjoy the mostly-level five-mile loop hike around stunning Bell Rock and Courthouse Buttes. Take your camera and make sure you've got plenty of space on the memory card. *Info*: 6.4 miles south of the 89/179 "Y" on 179. The trailhead and parking will be on your left. $5 Red Rock Pass required. You can buy passes at the trailhead or any of the Visitor's Centers.

If hiking isn't your thing, you should drive the **Red Rock Loop** west of town on 89A for spectacular views. You'll see the surreal formations of **Red Rock State Park** as well as the magnificent hoodoos and spires of **Cathedral Rock**. *Info*: The paved Red Rock Loop Road is located west of Sedona off of 89A. If you wish to enter Red Rock State Park there is a $5 entry fee.

After your hike or drive, consider having a meal in the **Village of Oak Creek**, just south of Sedona proper, on Highway 179. The **Desert Flour Bakery & Bistro** serves up awesome sandwiches and desserts (see *Sedona Sleeps & Eats*).

Even the most sedentary visitors should consider a visit to the **Chapel of the Holy Cross**. Built into the area's native red rock, the structure is **situated between two huge sandstone peaks**. The views from here make this a must-stop for people of any religion bent or calling. *Info*: Located on Chapel Road off of AZ 179 three miles south of the "Y." Tel. 928-282-4069. Open daily 9am-5pm. No admission fee but donations accepted.

Sedona was originally populated as an artist's colony, and there are plenty of **galleries** in town to vouch that it still is one. Many galleries, along with some nice boutiques, are concentrated in the **Tlaquepaque** shopping area about a half mile south of the "Y" on 179. Set up like a Mexican pueblo like under large sycamores, the area is worth a walk around even if you don't like to shop. You can also enjoy dinner at Tlaquepaque. For Mexican, try **El Rincon**, or for French-inspired Continental Cuisine there's **Rene** (see *Sedona Sleeps & Eats*).

If you're coming to or from Phoenix on your weekend, by sure to stop by the impressive ruins at **Montezuma Castle National Monument**. This cliff dwelling is an excellent example of Sinagua architecture. Built into the hollow of a vertical cliff, the **five-story dwelling** was constructed in the early part of the 12th century. *Info*: Exit 289, three miles off Interstate 17. Tel. 928-567-3322. www.nps.gov/moca/index.htm. Open daily 8am-5pm (6pm in summer). Admission $5 ages 16 and over.

ALTERNATIVE PLAN: For a different type of ad-**venture on the rocks**, try the extremely popular **Jeep Tours** (see *Sedona Best Activities*). After you strap yourself in, your guide will steer you up, down, and over what seem to be impossibly steep routes on the famous red rocks of the area. You'll get great views and a few surges of adrenaline as well.

A WONDERFUL WEEK IN NORTH-CENTRAL ARIZONA

With a week here there's time to do it all – take in the red rocks of Sedona, the cool, pine-covered mountains of Flagstaff, and the wonderful ruins, mining towns, and natural wonders of the rest of the region. This outdoor lover's paradise is just a few hours away from the Valley, yet is an entirely different world (and climate). Plus, it's only a little more than an hour from the Grand Canyon.

RECOMMENDED PLAN: Take two days in Flagstaff – one day for the in-town attractions and another for the Wupatki Loop. From Flagstaff head south to Sedona via Oak Creek Canyon. Spend two days exploring the red rocks and art galleries. Take another day to make the drive from Sedona to Jerome, hitting the attractions listed along the way. You'll want a day and a half in the Prescott so that you can see the sights of town and have the chance to get outside. Don't miss the surreal experimental village of Arcosanti on the way home.

Flagstaff

With an elevation of almost 7,000 feet, Flagstaff enjoys four distinct seasons. In the winter visitors come to **ski and snowboard** in the San Francisco Mountains at Snowbowl. In the summer Flagstaff is a wonderful escape from the intense Phoenix heat. Gorgeous colored leaves and stunning wildflower displays bring people to town in the fall and spring. Flagstaff is also the **gateway to the Grand Canyon**.

For a wonderful introduction to the entire Colorado Plateau region, head straight to the outstanding **Museum of Northern Arizona**. With exhibits that focus on the anthropology, biology, geology, and fine arts of the region, the museum offers something for everyone. They also offer various festivals through out the year **celebrating the Navajo, Hopi, and Hispanic cultures** of the area. Kids will enjoy the short hike through the woods to a little pond. *Info*: Three miles north of town on Highway 180 (3101 North Fort Valley Road.) Tel. 928-774-5213. www.musnaz.org. Open daily 9am-5pm. Admission $5 adults; $2 children 7-17.

Just a few miles up Highway 180 is **Arizona Snowbowl**, a year-round **escape for outdoor enthusiasts** but worth a visit even if all you do it take in the views. During the summer the resort's chairlift is used to carry visitors up the mountain to panoramic vistas at 11,500 feet. (It's **wonderfully cool** up there — take a jacket even in the summer.) There are also excellent **hikes** that start near the base of the chair lift and a **disc golf course**. During the winter you can enjoy **skiing and snowboarding** from the same spot. Great hikes near Snowbowl include:

• **Humphrey's Peak Trail** – Summit the highest point in Arizona at 12,633 feet. Difficult.
• **Kachina Trail** – One of the few trails that traverses the mountain instead of going straight up it. Moderate.
• **Veit Springs Loop Trail** – A wonderful walk through the aspens that includes a visit to an old homestead and views of pictographs. Easy.

Don't Miss...

• **Flagstaff** – Heritage Square; Museum of Northern Arizona; Snowbowl; Wupatki & Sunset Crater Volcano National Monuments; Riordan Mansion
• **Sedona** – Oak Creek Canyon; Tlaquepaque; Hiking, biking or driving through the red rocks
• **Prescott** – Courthouse Plaza, Whiskey Row, Granite Basin
• **Jerome**
• **Montezuma National Monument**

Info: Take Highway 180 seven miles north of Flagstaff to Snowbowl Road and continue up the mountain seven miles.

Tel. 928-779-1951. www.arizonasnowbowl.com. Costs and hours vary depending on activity.

Back in town, near the Northern Arizona University campus you can visit the beautiful **Riordan Mansion State Historic Park**. This 40-room mansion was built in 1904 by a family who made their fortune in lumbering. It's a wonderful example of **Arts and Crafts style architecture** that features log-slab siding, volcanic stone arches, and hand-split wooden shingles. Guided one-hour tours take you through the many rooms with original furnishings and artifacts. Kids might find it a bit slow, but most adults really enjoy it. *Info*: Half a mile north of the intersection of I-17 and I-40 at 1300 Riordan Ranch St. Tel. 928-779-4395. www.azstateparks.com/Parks/parkhtml/riordan.html. 10:30am-5:30pm daily (8:30am in summer.) $5 adults. $2.50 children under 17.

Good Eats Near Campus

As long as you're near the Northern Arizona University campus you might want to take a quick tour. Highlights of the campus include historic Old Main and Taylor Hall as well as the Cline Library. You can also grab a bite nearby at one of the inexpensive restaurants favored by students – Bunhuggers for burgers; El Charro for Mexican, or Alpine for pizza.

If you head up Milton Road from the Riordan Mansion, you'll see Mars Hill Road on the left. Take this road up to the popular **Lowell Observatory**, the place where the **planet Pluto was discovered**. You can tour during the day, when the astronomy exhibits and tours of the facilities are the main draws, or at night, when you can **peer through telescopes** at the night sky. Depending on the time of year, you may see the moon, planets, or globular and open star clusters through their 24-inch Clark Telescope. *Info*: 1400 West Mars Hill Road. Tel. 928-774-3358. www.lowell.edu. Open for both day and evening tours. Extended summer hours. Admission $5 adults. $2 children 5-17.

One of my favorite things to do in Flagstaff is simply hangout downtown on **Heritage Square**. It's a great place to get a feel for this crunchy mountain town. Everything about the square has significance, from the path detailing the history, biology, geology and anthropology of Flagstaff on a series of plaques to the redbrick railroad track design signifying the **importance of the railroad**. Even the benches in the Square are designed to represent Flagstaff history - the railroad, Lowell Observatory, the ranching and lumber industries and the Native American heritage. Check for free music and movie events during the summer. *Info*: Downtown on Aspen between San Francisco and Leroux Streets. www.heritagesquaretrust.org.

Those interested in the **botany** of the area will want to take a trip to the **Arboretum at Flagstaff**, located about seven miles south of Business I-40 via Woody Mountain Road. The collection includes mainly rare and endangered plant species, as well as one of the **largest collections of high country wildflowers** in America. Shaded walks, birds, a tranquil brook, fragrant butterfly garden and fantastic views of the San Francisco Peaks along a mile-long nature trail are some of the highlights.

Wupatki Loop
Some of the most fascinating attractions in the Flagstaff area aren't within the city limits, but on a loop route that covers a total of about 60 miles. The loop includes **well-preserved Native American ruins** and **amazing volcanic formations**.

Take US-89 12 miles north of Flagstaff and follow the signs to **Sunset Crater Volcano National Monument**. A massive volcanic eruption and extensive lava flow occurred here more than 900 years ago. Don't miss the self-guided **Bonito Lava Flow Trail** to experience the many different volcanic formations that remain a millennium after the 200-year long period of volcanic activity. The jagged black rocks stand out in start contrast to the red, yellow and orange shades of a **thousand-foot high cinder cone** beyond.

Continue on the loop road for ten miles to the **Wupatki National Monument**, once home to the ancient native Anasazi and Sinagua civilizations. Along the way you'll see some excellent views of the **Painted Desert** in the distance. Park at the visitor's center to tour the largest complex in the park, the Wupatki ruins. A trail

 leads down to a group of five ruins as well as to an amphi-theater used for ceremonial purposes and a ball court. Don't miss the **blow-hole at the end of the trail**. Natives believed this was where the earth breathed.

Other options in the park include the Lomaki Pueblo Trail, an easy half-mile walk, and the Wukoki, Citadel, and Nalakihu Pueblos, which are also reached by short quarter-mile trails. *Info*: Off US-89 north of Flagstaff. Tel. 928-679-2365. www.nps.gov/ wupa/index.htm. Open daily 9am-5pm. $5 adults 17 and older.

Walnut Canyon National Monument
If you haven't gotten enough of native cultures you can add a side trip to Walnut Canyon on the way back to Flagstaff. This was home to an Indian culture known as the Sinagua. Here today are the remains of the community they developed between about 1125 and 1250 AD. You'll walk through **impressive homes built beneath overhanging cliffs** in the canyon's walls. The paved trail is steep, but worth the effort. *Info*: 7.5 miles east of Flagstaff on I-40 (exit 204.) Tel. 928-526-3367. www.nps.gov/waca. Open daily 9am-5pm. $5 adults 17 and older.

Sedona & Oak Creek Canyon
Sedona, with its surreal red rocks and new-age "vortex sites" is the perfect place to play outside all day and then dine and sleep in luxury.

Heading south from Flagstaff, be sure to take AZ-89A instead of I-17. 89A **winds for a memorable 25 miles** down the impressive Oak Creek Canyon from the southern edge of the Colorado Plateau to the town of Sedona. Featuring sheer cliffs, pine forests that descend to red rocks, and **impressive deep gorges**, it's a fantastic drive. Don't miss the **Oak Creek Vista** point on your way down for both impressive views of the canyon and an opportunity to shop at a Native American Co-op market.

If you like to hike, plan on stopping 17.5 miles south of Flagstaff at the **West Fork Hiking Trail**. One of the most popular hikes in the region, the trails meander along, over, and through the creek sheltered by soaring red rock cliffs. Wear shoes you don't mind getting wet.

Slide Rock State Park

As you approach Sedona on 89-A, you'll see the park on your right. No matter how hot it is outside, the **cool waters of the natural** park **pools** at Slide Rock are a refreshing treat. The smooth rock water slides are a hit for kids of all ages. The park was named by Life Magazine as **one of American's 10 most beautiful swimming holes**. When apples are in season you can pick them from the park's orchard. *Info*: 7 miles north of

> ## Picnic Time!
>
> Pack a picnic lunch when you leave Flagstaff so that you can eat al fresco at the Slide Rock State Park after your swim.

Sedona on AZ-89A. Tel. 928-282-3034. www.pr.state.az.us/Parks/parkhtml/sliderock.html. Open daily 8am-5pm. (7pm in summer). $10 per vehicle.

Downtown Sedona

Shoppers will be thrilled with the options in Sedona. Try **Main Street** for more commercial items like t-shirts and Native America curios, or the **delightful shops of Tlaquepaque for art galleries and boutiques**. Tlaquepaque, created as an "arts & crafts village," was designed to look like a Mexican pueblo. With pleasant courtyards, trickling fountains, and cobblestone pathways, it's been a Sedona landmark since the 1970s. *Info*: Located on 179 just south of the "Y." Tel. 928-282-4838. Open daily 10am-5pm.

Continuing a few miles south on 179, you'll see the **Chapel of the Holy Cross**. Built between two huge sandstone peaks, the chapel offers **splendid panoramic views**. Even the nonreligious will be moved by the grandeur of the site. *Info*: Located on Chapel Road off of AZ 179 three miles south of the "Y." Tel. 928-282-4069. Open daily 9am-5pm. No admission fee but donations accepted.

The Great Outdoors
Whether you hike, bike, jeep, or just drive, you've got to spend some time exploring the red rocks that make Sedona so unique. One of my favorite hikes for visitors is accessed by heading south on 179 towards the Village of Oak Creek to **Bell Rock**. You can simply walk out to Bell Rock (easy option), or enjoy the mostly-level five-mile loop hike around stunning Bell Rock and Courthouse Buttes. *Info*: 6.4 miles south of the 89/179 "Y" on 179. The trailhead and parking will be on your left. $5 Red Rock Pass required. You can buy passes at the trailhead or any of the Visitor's Centers.

Other memorable Sedona hikes are:
• **Boyton Canyon**
• **Airport Mesa**
• **Devil's Bridge**

If hiking isn't your thing, you should drive the **Red Rock Loop** west of town on 89A for spectacular views. You'll see the surreal formations of **Red Rock State Park** as well as the magnificent hoodoos and spires of **Cathedral Rocks**. (Cathedral Rocks is supposed to be one of the most photographed spots in the US.) *Info*: The paved Red Rock Loop Road is located west of Sedona off of 89A. If you wish to enter Red Rock State Park there is a $5 entry fee.

Those wanting a little **off-road 4x4 adventure** should line up a jeep tour. The guides are quite knowledgeable and the experience of driving up, down, and over such steep stretches of slick rock is unforgettable (see Sedona Best Activities).

Golfers will love combining their favorite sport with Sedona's incredible scenery. Try the **Sedona Golf Resort** (Tel. 800-426-6148). Look smart on the par 3 hole #10, one of the most photographed holes in Arizona.

The Great Indoors

While Sedona is known for its outdoor pursuits, it's also a **mecca for spa-goers**. The new-age flute music that accompanies most massages somehow seems very appropriate in Sedona. The **Enchantment Resort, Adobe Grand Villas, and Sedona Rouge** all offer a full menu of spa treatments (see *Sedona Sleeps & Eats*).

Prescott/Jerome Area

If you have time, it's definitely worth taking two days to explore this area. You'll discover **historic mining towns,** wonderful **natural scenery,** and **real cowboy culture**.

Sedona to Jerome

This trip will take from a half to full day depending on which sights pique your interest and whether or not you take the train. The entire distance from Sedona to Jerome is only 30 miles. (Jerome is the highlight of the route for most people.)

Eat Well in Sedona

Some of the best bets for haute cuisine can be found at the area's resorts. L'Auberge de Sedona and the Yavapai Restaurant at the Enchantment Resort offer the highest level of gourmet cuisine in the city, but they are closely followed by The Gallery at Oak Creek at Amara and Reds at the Sedona Rouge.

Take 89A West miles to Cottonwood, where you'll find the **Dead Horse Ranch State Park** off of North 10th St. The park's Verde River is **one of the Arizona desert's last free-flowing rivers**. It sustains a large regional wildlife population and a lush riparian community in the **dense forest along its banks**. Visitors enjoy hiking along the river, bird watching, canoeing, picnicking, fishing, or just sticking their feet in the cool water. (Don't worry, there are no dead horses there now. When owners bought the place in the '40s there was a dead horse by the road. The kids in the family kept calling it the Dead Horse Ranch and the name stuck.) *Info*: 675 Dead Horse Ranch Road off of North 10th St. in Cottonwood. Tel. 928-634-5283. www.pr.state.az.us/Parks/parkhtml/deadhorse.html. Open daily. $4 per vehicle.

From Cottonwood, take AZ260 towards Clarkdale. Just before you enter Clarkdale there will be signs for the **Tuzigoot National Monument**. Meaning "crooked water" in Apache, Tuzigoot is what remains of a **12ᵗʰ century Sinaguan village** constructed atop a ridge that rises above the Verde Valley. An easy trail leads to the visitor's center and loops around the ruins. You can climb up to the top to get a good view of the entire ruins and the Verde Valley beyond. *Info*: Off AZ289 near Clarkdale. Tel. 928-634-5564. Open 8am-5pm daily (7pm in summer). $5 per adult over 17.

Both train buffs and nature enthusiasts will want to stop in Clarkdale, as it's the starting point for a scenic ride on the **Verde Canyon Railroad**. By taking the train you are able to **traverse a portion of the Sycamore Wilderness that is not accessible by road**. The trip takes about four hours and includes several deep canyon trestle crossings. You can see wildlife (including deer and bald eagles), as well as the remains of many Sinaguan villages. The train features open and closed cars and there is food service on board. *Info*: Tel. 800-320-0718. www.verdecanyonrr.com. Contact the railroad for departure times. One or two trains depart daily depending on demand. $55 Adult (coach), $35 child (coach.) First class seating also available.

Jerome

About five miles beyond Clarkdale you'll rejoin AZ 89A for the final couple of miles into **Jerome**. The enjoyable burgh, once a booming city, boasted a population of 15,000 and was known as the Wickedest Town of the West at the height of its copper mining days. With the closure of the last mine in the 1950s, Jerome almost became a ghost town. It has enjoyed a rebirth of late however and is home to a **number of art galleries, shops and restaurants** to serve the growing visitor population. The streets of the **picturesque town** wind up and down Cleopatra Hill, and its buildings, many constructed in the late 1800s, seem to **perch precariously** on the brink.

My favorite thing to do in Jerome is simply walk the streets, enjoy the views, and then have a nice, long lunch or dinner at either the **Haunted Hamburger** or the **Asylum at the Jerome Grand Hotel** on Hill Street (see *Jerome Sleeps & Eats*).

If you've still got some touring in you, the Douglas Mansion at the **Jerome State Historic Park** is worth a visit. One of the most interesting features of the museum is a large three-dimensional model of the town as it appeared in its heyday, including a cutaway of the mines. *Info*: Just off 89A in Jerome. Tel. 928-634-5381. www.pr.state.az.us/Parks/parkhtml/jerome.html. Open daily 8am-5pm. $4 adults. $3 children 7-13.

If you end up in Jerome in the evening, I would suggest spending the night so that you can enjoy the lovely drive down to Prescott during the light of day.

Prescott
Prescott, 35 miles past Jerome on AZ-89A, began as a mining town in the middle of the 19th century. Retirees and vacationers flock here now for the **mild weather and small-town feel**. Prescott embraces its **cowboy history**, which you'll see in many of the area attractions.

Begin your tour of Prescott's downtown at the lovely tree-covered **Courthouse Plaza**, the center of civic life. Both visitors and locals set up blankets under the huge shade trees and enjoy the many fairs here on the weekends. There are several statues on the grounds, including **impressive Bucky O'Neill Monument**, which honors the first volunteer in the Spanish-American War and the man who founded the Rough Riders of Teddy Roosevelt fame.

Near the Courthouse and along Gurley St. you'll find the **historic portion of town**. Prescott has over 500 buildings listed in the National Register of Historic Places, which is more than any other community in the state. The greatest concentration of shops, especially antique dealers, is located along a two-block stretch of Cortez St., north of Courthouse Plaza. **Whiskey Row**, located off the plaza on the 100 block of

Let Loose at Matt's!

Matt's Saloon, 112 Montezuma, is the place for honky-tonkin' once the sun goes down. Whether you're a real cowboy or a wannabe, this is the spot for two-stepping, pool shooting, and beer drinking.

Montezuma Street, was where the miners came to let off a little steam. Locals and tourists do the same nowadays in the many cowboy saloons on this stretch. (There are ice cream shops and art galleries here as well.) Most of the buildings were constructed between 1900-1905 after a fire wiped out the first version of Whiskey Row.

The **Sharlot Hall Museum**, on Gurley, consists of three historic buildings that are furnished in the manner similar to when they were first built. The **Governor's Mansion** is a highlight with an excellent display of western transportation that included a stage-coach and Conestoga wagon. *Info*: 415 Gurley St. Tel. 928-445-3122. www.sharlot.org. Open daily 10am-4pm (5pm in summer.) No admission fee but donation requested.

Cowboy Art Collection

If you're a fan of cowboy art, the **Phippen Museum** seven miles north of town on AZ-89, has a sizable collection of works by famous Western artists. Tel. 928-778-1385. www.phippenartmuseum.org.

Outdoor Activities in the Prescott Area
The climate is what draws many people to Prescott. When it's smoking hot in Phoenix you can enjoy wonderful hikes and bike rides here. The gorgeous **Granite Basin Recreation Area**, out Iron Springs Road, is a must for hikers and mountain bikers. The **massive granite boulders**, smoothed by weather and time, look like statues reflected in **Granite Basin Lake**. Enjoy loop hikes through the pines or out and backs.

Another fantastic granite outcropping can be found five miles north of town on AZ 89 at **Granite Dells** and lovely **Watson Lake**. It looks like a giant took some handfuls of marbles (i.e. smoothed boulders) and threw them all around the water. The **Peavine Trail** is a good one in this area.

One of Prescott's better-known natural features is a rugged granite outcropping known as the **Thumb Butte**. Take Gurley three miles out (becomes Thumb Butte Road) and enjoy a two-mile loop hike up to through the **Ponderosa pines** to the base of the butte for great views of the Prescott National Forest.

I-17 Corridor

There are a few sights that don't fit neatly into one of the town descriptions, but are worth a stop if you are coming to or from Phoenix. The best of these is the impressive ruins at **Montezuma Castle National Monument**. This cliff dwelling is an excellent example of Sinagua architecture. Built into the hollow of a vertical cliff, the **five-story dwelling** was constructed in the early part of the 12th century. The sight is located along a pleasant creek and is well-worth a visit. *Info*: Exit 289, three miles off Interstate 17. Tel. 928-567-3322. www.nps.gov/moca/index.htm. Open daily 8am-5pm (6pm in summer). Admission $5 ages 16 and over.

Closer to Phoenix, at the Cordes Junction turn off to Prescott, is the unusual **Arcosanti**. Arcosanti is the brainchild of renowned architect Paolo Soleri – his vision includes a complete **urban community for 5,000 totally in harmony with nature**. Encompassing more than 4,000 acres of natural area, the 15-acre townsite is intended to be a community for working artists. It has been under construction for many years and will probably never be completed, but it remains an interesting place to visit. There is even lodging available if you really want to **experience archology first hand**. *Info*: Off exit 262 on I-17. Follow signs for three miles down dirt road. Tel. 928-632-7135. Open 9am-5pm. Guided one-hour tours are offered every half-hour from 10am-4pm. $5 fee for tour.

6. THE GRAND CANYON

Any words used to describe the Grand Canyon are insufficient to do it proper justice. The same is true for pictures and video, because these mediums cannot capture the depth and layers you see when standing on the canyon's rim. If you've never been before, this will be a very memorable outing.

The **Grand Canyon National Park** covers 1900 square miles and is 277 miles long. The **Colorado River** divides the **North Rim** from the **South Rim**. Although it only averages about 15 miles across from one rim to the other, the canyon isn't traversed by any roads. So, if you have to travel by car from the South to North Rims it's a 210-mile drive. The **South Rim is much more accessible** from major population centers and is, therefore, the focus of the one-day and weekend itineraries.

ONE GREAT DAY AT THE GRAND CANYON

Yes, it's just a big hole in the ground, but it's the most impressive and beautiful big hole you'll ever see. Even if all you have is one day, this is the single most important and majestic sight in Arizona, so make sure you see it while you're here.

Start from the entrance station on US 180/AZ 64. After paying your entry free, you'll follow the gently curving road through a few miles of forest. You'll be saying to yourself, "Where's the canyon?" Actually, you won't see it until you're right upon it. Continue straight at the junction in the road to the first viewing area at **Mather Point.**

This is your first look into the canyon and for that reason alone it will be **simply unforgettable.** Here, and at every other stop along the rim, you'll begin to understand that part of the wonderment that every visitor to the canyon feels is caused not only by the majestic beauty of the scene, but also by the sheer scale. The **canyon simply dwarfs everything** – people, cars, even the few building on the canyon's rim. It can make you feel very small and insignificant and does justice to the marvels of nature.

A little further along the road, take the short cutoff to the **hauntingly beautiful** view from **Yavapai Point.** The small **Yavapai Museum** offers some interesting information on the canyon's geology.

After Yavapai Point you'll soon reach the **Grand Canyon Village** area, which is where

Walk this Way

Walkers should take note that the entire rim from Mather Point to Hermits Rest at the end of the West Rim Drive is accessible by a continuous trail. The portion from Yavapai to Maricopa is paved. It is the easiest trail in the park and the only one that doesn't require a descent into the canyon.

the majority of services, including hotels, are located. Be advised that it is among the most crowded portions of the park at any time. It is also the location of the park's **Visitor Center**, a good place to see some interesting exhibits on the park's natural and human history and well as to get information from the always helpful and friendly rangers.

If you're not spending the night at one of the hotels on the rim, take some time now to walk along the rim trail in front of the village. Don't miss the **Kolb Studio**, built by two photographers early in the 1900s on the edge of the canyon rim. There are some great views out the studio window.

If you are going to do any hiking into the canyon, one excellent option here is the **Bright Angel Trail**. It is the same trail that is used by the mule trips. (By the way, mules always have the right of way should you encounter them on the trail.) The trail descends to the Colorado River by a **series of steep switchbacks**. It is not for the faint of heart, although inexperienced hikers often enjoy going part of the way down just to get the feel of descending into the canyon. Be sure to take plenty of water.

Geology Lesson

The walls of the Grand Canyon are a veritable museum of natural history that span about one half of the earth's almost five billion year existence. The forces of erosion, primarily the cutting action of the Colorado River, but also wind and rain, have exposed many colorful layers of rock strata. The oldest of the 12 layers (about 1.7 billion years) is at the bottom and the youngest (only 250 million years) is at the top.

A warning is in order for all canyon trails. **Never attempt to reach the Colorado River at the bottom of the canyon and try to get back in the same day**. People have died from exhaustion trying to do so.

The South Rim is divided into West and East drives. Take the **West Rim** route from the Village. If you did not hike, take the time to stop at the **Hopi**, **Maricopa**, and **Pima** Points. If you took a hike and are short on time, don't miss the West Rim's best spot – **The Abyss**. Here the Great Mojave

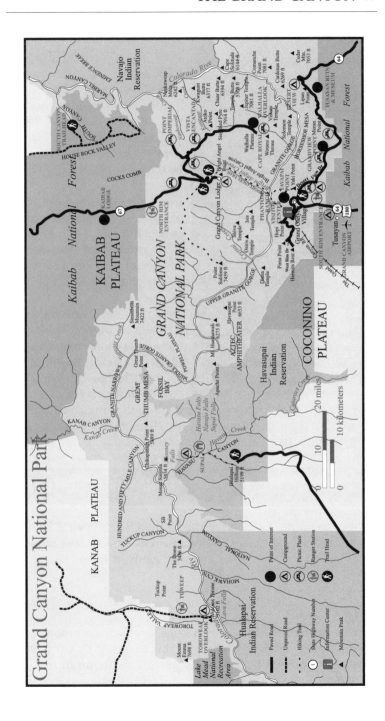

ALTERNATIVE PLAN: Some people prefer to see the **canyon by air**, which has certain advantages for those with limited time. You can certainly cover more ground by plane than you would by car. While flights have been **restricted due to the noise pollution they cause**, they are still available. Try **Grand Canyon Airlines** (Tel. 800-528-2413. www.grandcanyonairlines.com) for half-day trips from the Grand Canyon Airport. Tours start at $110. They also have a very popular daylong tour that includes a canyon over-flight as well as a **raft float** through part of the canyon on the Colorado River.

Wall of the canyon has an almost **sheer vertical drop of 3,000 feet**. This provides visitors with a clear view of the Tonto Platform within the canyon and the Colorado River. The Abyss is the only place on the West Rim that the river can be seen.

Don't miss the amazing colors of sunset if you are staying in or near the park overnight. The **most spectacular sunsets** can be seen from Hopi and Pima points on the West Rim.

After your day of activity you'll be ready for dinner. The hands down **best choice** for that is the **El Tovar Dining Room** at the El Tovar Hotel. The gorgeous Arts & Crafts architecture from the early 1900s is a perfect compliment to the fantastic food and service. Make reservations well in advance and you'll be one happy camper (see *Grand Canyon Sleeps & Eats*).

A FANTASTIC GRAND CANYON WEEKEND

With an entire weekend at the Grand Canyon you'll have time to cover the **entire South Rim** as well as take some **hikes** and just sit and soak in the beauty of the scene.

Friday Evening

Because the **South Rim** is the most accessible from urban areas, I'm assuming for the purposes of this itinerary that it is your destination. Hopefully you'll get up to the canyon in time for sunset. If so, drive straight to either **Hopi, Pima, Desert View, Lipan** or **Mojave** point for **spectacular views of the sunset colors** off the canyon walls.

Watch for elk on the road on your way back to the **Grand Canyon Village** and your hotel. After checking in, head to the **Arizona Room** for some tender, sizzling steaks. They also have menu alternatives for non-meat eaters (See *Grand Canyon Sleeps & Eats*).

Saturday
If you're an early bird, I suggest getting up and at'em for **sunrise** at **Lipan, Mather, Yaki,** or **Yavapai** points. Even if all you do is sit on the rim trail in front of the Grand Canyon Village, sunrise at the canyon is a special moment.

If you're physically up for the challenge, a **hike in the canyon is simply an unforgettable experience**. You won't have time to go all the way down and up in a day (don't even think about trying it – idiots have died that way), but you can get in as long an out-and-back hike as you can handle. I suggest the **Bright Angel, Kaibab** or **Grandview Trails**. Be sure you have food, water, and proper clothing before you start. Park concessionaires offer guided hikes of different areas of the park if you're not up for doing it on your own.

If hiking is not your thing, hop in your car (or the park shuttle depending on the time of the year) and head out to the west section of the South Rim. While I recommend stopping at all points along the trail, if you go to only one, don't miss **The Abyss**. It's the lone spot on the west rim that you can see the Colorado River as well as sheer vertical drops of 3,000 feet. At **Powell Point** there is a monument to explorer John Wesley Powell. At the end of the west rim you'll arrive to **Hermit's Rest**, so called because a French-Canadian named Louis Boucher lived a solitary life here in the 1890s.

Take a Box Lunch

Arrange a box lunch from your hotel so that you can eat your afternoon meal at one of the viewpoints. There's no better seat in town.

Return to the Village after lunch for some down time to enjoy the canyon. Explore the **path along the rim**, visit the **Kolb Studio**, and just take a moment to let the beauty of the canyon work into your psyche. Besides the size, what is most awesome about the canyon is the wonderful array of colors in the rock. No two places are alike and even the same place can change radically from one moment to another depending upon how the sunlight plays on the rock face.

By far the best option for dinner is the wonderful **El Tover Dining Room** in the El Tovar Hotel. Call in advance for reservations so that you can enjoy gourmet dining in the most historic hotel in the park.

Sunday
Today you'll take another hike, if that's your pleasure, and then **exit the park via the East Rim Drive**. The East Rim Drive covers a one-way distance of 23 miles. The less traveled East Rim has its overlooks spaced further apart than the West Rim and most of them are reached by spur roads of about a mile in length. Many of the viewpoints on the East Rim afford more spectacular vistas than the West Rim, so don't miss them.

ALTERNATIVE PLAN: If you can manage the hike or mule ride, an **overnight trip at the bottom of the canyon** is unforgettable. **Phantom Ranch** (see *Grand Canyon Sleeps & Eats*) has a few rustic individual cabins and two dorm-style ones. The food down there is excellent. It's best to make reservations far in advance, but you can always check for cancellations.

Yaki Point has some of the **best canyon views** of any overlook and is also the beginning of the **South Kaibab Trail**, which reaches Phantom Ranch and the river by a different route than the more popular Bright Angel Trail.

You'll want to stop at both **Moran** and **Lipan Points** for different perspectives than offered on the West Rim overlooks. You're looking back into the canyon more than down upon it. This affords a **greater appreciation of the vastness** of the canyon because you can see the different layers within it.

Finally, don't miss the **Desert View overlook**. From this point you can see a truly spectacular panorama that includes, besides the canyon itself, the **Colorado River**, colorful **Vermilion Cliffs**, the distant **San Francisco Peaks**, and a portion of the **Painted Desert**.

A Great Sunday Hike

The **Grandview Trail**, off Grandview Point on the East Rim, is an excellent day-hike as it doesn't go all the way to the bottom of the canyon. Instead, it leads to **colorful Horseshoe Mesa**. (This doesn't mean it isn't strenuous, however.)

ALTERNATIVE PLAN: Rafting the Colorado River through the Grand Canyon is an unforgettable experience that takes days. You can get a taste of that with a one-day **smooth water float from the Glen Canyon Dam** outside of Page, Arizona to Lee's Ferry, where the park officially starts. Call Aramark-Wilderness River Adventures (Tel. 928-645-3279) for reservations and information. You may also make arrangements through Grand Canyon National Park Lodges for transportation from the South Rim to Page. Call 303-297-2757 for more information.

After this you'll leave the park and continue along AZ64 to Cameron. Stop for dinner at the historic **Cameron Trading Post** to end your wonderful weekend (see *Grand Canyon Sleeps & Eats*).

A WONDERFUL WEEK AT THE GRAND CANYON

With an entire week at the canyon you'll have time to explore both the South and North Rims, giving you a unique perspective on this natural wonder.

RECOMMENDED PLAN: Spend two days at the South Rim so that you have time to visit the East and West Rims as well as the Grand Canyon Village. Take a day to drive from the South to the North Rim and then another two days to explore the North Rim. With a week you'll also have time to overnight in the canyon or take a short flat-water float trip if you're the active type.

South Rim
The South Rim is sub-divided into the **West and East Rim Drives**, with the **Grand Canyon Village** separating the two. During the summer months the West Rim Drive is closed to private vehicles, so you must either walk or take the free open-air tram shuttle, which operates at frequent intervals throughout the day.

Don't Miss...

• South Rim (West Section) – The Abyss Overlook; a meal at El Tovar; the Visitor's Center
• South Rim (East Section) – Yaki, Moran, Lipan, and Desert View Overlooks
• North Rim – Bright Angel Point, Cape Royal, Grand Canyon Lodge
• Hiking into the canyon if you're up for it physically

West Rim Drive
Arriving to the park on US-180/AZ-64, you'll want to stop at the first view point — **Mather Point**. Not the premier view in the park, it's special to many because it offers the first look into the majestic canyon. A little further along the road is the turn off to **Yavapai Point**, which is also home to the small **Yavapai Museum**. Walk through the museum, which focuses on the canyon's geology.

If you've got the time and the stamina, there is a trail that leads along the canyon rim from Mather Point to Hermit's Rest. This is the **only flat trail in the park,** so if you want to hike a little but can't handle steep inclines, this is the trail for you.

Grand Canyon Village

Soon after leaving Yavapai point you'll come to the **Grand Canyon Village,** where the majority of services and hotels are located. This is also where you'll find the informative **Visitor's Center,** a good place to see exhibits on the park's natural and human history. This is also **where the shuttle service begins**.

The **Kolb Studio,** built literally at the edge of the canyon by two photographers, has some great views out the studio windows. It's also a good place to escape from the elements for a few minutes as it's nice and warm in the winter and cool in the summer.

The Village is also where the **Bright Angel Trail** starts. This steep trail leads down to Phantom Ranch at the bottom of the canyon. You can hike part of the way down the trail for an interesting day hike, or, if you're prepared and have a permit, hike down and spend the night at the bottom of the canyon.

Continuing along the eight-mile West Rim Drive you'll come to the **Hopi, Maricopa,** and **Pima** Points. They are all beautiful, but the best of the lot is the next overlook, called **The Abyss.** At The Abyss, the Great Mojave Wall drops a sheer 3,000 feet, providing you with a **clear view of the Colorado River.** The West Rim ends at **Hermit's Rest,** which is the start of the strenuous 17-mile round-trip **Hermit Trail**.

Reading Material

In 1869, one-armed John Wesley Powell and a small group journeyed a thousand miles on the Colorado River and through the entire Grand Canyon, exploring previously unknown lands. Read about it in Powell's excellent *Exploration of the Colorado River and Its Canyons.* Then, in the late 1800s, Fred Harvey began transporting visitors to the canyon. His adventurous employees are profiled in *The Harvey Girls: Women Who Opened the West.*

East Rim Drive

The East Rim Drive covers a one-way distance of 23 miles. The overlooks are spaced further apart than on the West Rim and most of them are reached by spur roads of about a mile in length. **Yaki Point** has some of the best canyon views of any overlook and is also the beginning of the **South Kaibab Trail**. The wonderful trail leads down to Phantom Ranch along some beautiful ridge overlooks.

The next overlook is the **Grandview Point**. The six-mile roundtrip **Grandview Trail** is a great day hike because it doesn't go to the bottom of the canyon, but rather to Horseshoe Mesa. Even so, it's a steep, hard trail.

Sunset & Sunrise

Don't miss either sunrise or sunset in the park, as they are truly spectacular. The sunrises are best at Lipan, Mather, Yaki, and Yavapai Points, while the sunsets are most spectacular at Desert View, Hopi, Lipan, Mojave, and Pima Points.

Both **Moran** and **Lipan** points offer a different perspective than the West Rim Overlooks, as you'll be looking back into the canyon more than down upon it. I like it because it affords views of the many different layers. You can also see how the gorge that contains the Colorado River is actually a canyon within a canyon.

A worthwhile sight on the East Rim is the **Tusayan Ruin**, the small but interesting remains of a prehistoric pueblo. There is also an interpretive museum.

The **grand finale** is the spectacular **Desert View**. A wonderful panorama spot, you'll have views of the canyon, the Colorado River, the Vermilion Cliffs, the San Francisco Peaks, and a portion of the Painted Desert. A re-creation of an Anasazi tower, called the **Watchtower**, was built here early in the 1900s. You can climb up top for even better views.

Mule Trips & Tours

People have been riding mules to the bottom of the Grand Canyon for more than 100 years. **Mules are preferable to horses** because they are more sure-footed and have a much better temperament for the task. Be aware though that you will be spending a lot of time in the saddle. This is a very popular way to see the canyon, so it is suggested that **reservations be made six to eight months in advance.** There are three different trips.  One is an overnight trip to the Phantom Ranch, while another is a three-day journey. The last, a **one-day trip, is the most popular.** Departing daily from both the North and South Rims, it descends over 3,000 feet to the canyon's Tonto Platform (not all the way to the Colorado River.) The round-trip takes about seven hours. *Info*: Tel. 888-297-2757. www.grandcanyonlodges.com/Mule-Trips-716.html. $135 for one-day trip. Rider qualifications include weight limit (200 pounds), height limit (must be at least 4'7") and English fluency.

Grand Canyon Railway
To feel like you've stepped back in time, take the train from Williams to the Grand Canyon. Williams, 31-miles west of Flagstaff on I-40, is the origin of the famous **Grand Canyon Railway**. You'll start in a historic depot, built in 1910, and then board ornate coaches for the ride to the rim. Once there, you'll have 3.5 hours to either tour the rim by bus or explore around on your own. The roundtrip trip takes about eight hours. During your time on the train there is often music and entertainment. In the winter the train is transformed to the magical Polar Express. Reservations are recommended well in advance. *Info*: Tel. 800-843-8724. www.thetrain.com. From $75 for adults and $25 for children under 10.

Driving Route to the North Rim
While some people will be lucky enough to hike down the south side and back up to the North Rim, most visitors to the North Rim end up driving the 210 miles around the canyon from side to side. A good portion of the drive along AZ 64 to Cameron parallels the **Little Colorado River Gorge**. Along the road you'll pass several

trading posts. Be on the lookout for them even if you aren't in the market for shopping because it is near these posts that **short spur roads lead near the edge of the gorge**. Brief walks will take you to the precipice. Be extra careful because some of the overlooks are not fenced in – hold onto your children!

At Cameron you can visit the historic **Cameron Trading Post**. Have a meal here, do some shopping, or just browse the **incredible art gallery** with rare and unique Native American pieces. From here, take 89 north to Bitter Spring and then follow 89A to AZ67 to the North Rim.

The drive from Bitter Spring to Marble Canyon is highly scenic with broad vistas of huge red sandstone cliffs surrounding an immense and equally colorful valley. **Marble Canyon**, which is actually located in a narrow strip of the eastern edge of Grand Canyon National Park, is a scene of great beauty that **definitely merits a stop**. Park at either end and walk over the **Navajo Bridge** which spans the Colorado River **over a deep gorge** that drops almost 800 feet to the water. With wonderful views of the gorge and river as well as the breathtaking backdrop of giant red sandstone cliffs, this is a **great place for a picnic lunch**.

Once you cross the river, you're in a part of the state known as the **Arizona Strip**. Before the construction of the Navajo Bridge, this portion of Arizona was physically cut off from the rest of the state. Highway 89A travels for 40 miles from here to Jacob Lake, climbing from monolithic red mountains to **a more forested area**. At Jacob Lake head south for 40 miles on AZ 67 through the thick greenery of the Kaibab National Forest until you reach the entrance to the North Rim.

North Rim
Only about 10% of the visitors to the South Rim make it to the North Rim, but those who do find the experience highly rewarding. The **Grand Canyon Lodge** is the hub of all activities here. Take note that the North Rim is **generally only open from the middle of May to the middle of October** depending on the amount of snow. There are guided bus tours of the North Rim

should you choose not to drive and **one bus a day that travels from rim to rim**.

Some of the **best sights on the North Rim** are located right by the lodge, not the least of which is the spectacular panorama available from the veranda of the lodge itself. But the real **highlight** of a North Rim visit involves taking the half-mile long **Bright Angel Point Trail** from directly behind the lodge out to **Bright Angel Point**. The trail is easy, but is entirely on an extremely narrow ridge that juts out into the canyon. There's a **delightfully dizzying drop on either side**.

If you want to hike, the **Transept Trail** stretches along the North Rim's edge for about three miles from the lodge area to the campground, while the **North Kaibab Trail** descends to the canyon floor at Phantom Ranch (an overnight trip).

There are some excellent vista points on the North Rim. Start with the 8,830-foot **Point Imperial**. This is the **highest point on either rim** and the view is dramatic and beautiful. You'll gaze eastward into a portion of the canyon not visible from anywhere on the South Rim's road system. It is wilder here as the colorful rocks are more intertwined with vegetation. Clusters **of huge ponderosa pines and other trees appear as tiny green specks** in the distance – an unforgettable sight.

The Cape Royal Drive also has some great sights. These include the **Vista Encantadora** and the **Walhalla Overlook**. Be sure to also take the short trail to the **Angel's Window**, a large rock formation where erosion has carved out a giant hole.

Finally you'll arrive to **Cape Royal**, where one of the most colorful of all Grand Canyon vistas awaits. You'll see the

Get Off the Beaten Path

If you've already experienced the main part of the canyon, you might want to explore to the west, where you'll be much more off the beaten path. Havasu Falls is for the physically fit, while the Grand Canyon Skywalk is for anyone not afraid of heights.

Granite Gorge, as well as **Wotan's Throne**, a giant rock formation rising proudly from a plateau within the depths of the canyon. You'll also catch a **panoramic view of canyon, forest, and distant mountains** that is simply mesmerizing.

Havasu Falls

If you see a picture of **lovely blue-green waterfalls**, and the picture is in Arizona, it is probably from Havasu Falls. Located in a remote region of the western section of the Grand Canyon, the falls are **accessible only by hiking, horseback riding, or helicopter**. If you've got the time and the stamina, it is definitely worth hiking the trip.

First you must **hike eight miles** down the Hualapai Trail to the village of Supai, where there is a small store and a lodge (Tel. 928-448-2111). If you are camping, you must hike two miles further to the campgrounds. The falls are in this area as well. Havasu, Mooeney, and Navaho Falls are all **great photo spots as well as wonderful places to take a dip**. *Info*: Havasupai Tourist Enterprise, Supai, AZ 86435. Tel 928-448-2121. www.kaibab.org/supai. $30 entry fee and additional charges for camping ($10) and the lodge ($135.)

Grand Canyon West Skywalk

A new diversion along the Grand Canyon is the Grand Canyon Skywalk, a **glass bridge suspended at the edge of the canyon** 4,000 above the Colorado River. Slated for completion in late 2006, it will certainly draw those interested in a thrill. Made out of more than one million pounds of steel, the bridge will supposedly be able to **sustain winds in excess of 100 miles per hour** from 8 different directions, as well as an 8.0 magnitude earthquake within 50 miles.

Other things to do in the area include visiting a "Wild West Town", an "Indian Village", as well as **Hummer and helicopter tours**. The whole area is mainly set up for **visitors from Las Vegas**, so it's got a bit of that Vegas feel to it all, even though there are currently relatively few visitors. There's a lodge here as well *Info*: Tel. 877-716- 9378. 120 miles east of Las Vegas or 80 miles northwest of Kingman, AZ. www.destinationgrandcanyon.com.

7. NORTHEASTERN ARIZONA

This vast, sparsely populated region has been home to both the Navajo and Hopi peoples for centuries. The expansive Navajo Nation covers most of the region. Blessed with impressive sandstone rock formations, beautiful canyons, and well-preserved ruins, the Navajo Nation is also fascinating from a cultural standpoint. Equally fascinating is the small Hopi Reservation surrounded entirely by the Navajo Nation. You can visit the three mesas that the Hopi have occupied for centuries, learn about their way of life, and have the opportunity to buy incredible hand-crafted art.

In the northwestern corner of the region you'll find the impressive Lake Powell, part of the Glen Canyon National Recreation Area, and a boater's dream.

ONE GREAT DAY IN NORTHEASTERN ARIZONA

The distances between sights are far in this part of the state, but the pay-off is some of the most incredible landscapes in the country. From soaring canyon walls to nature-sculpted rock formations, the wonders present here will stay with you forever.

Begin your day at the memorable **Canyon de Chelly National Monument** near Chinle. The canyon, while not as deep or dramatic as the Grand Canyon, is beautiful because of the **deep rust color of the smooth and sheer rocky walls**. These walls, contrasted with shimmering cottonwood trees and green Navajo farms, create a special landscape not to be missed. The canyon is also important historically because of the many ruins tucked into these extraordinary cliffs.

Start with a **half-day tour into the canyon**. While it is possible to drive your own four-wheel drive vehicle as long as you have a Navajo guide with you, I highly suggest hiring a jeep or truck designed especially for the trip. Not only is the deep sand very difficult to navigate, it's also just much nicer to have somebody else drive you around so that you can **sit back in the open air and take in the sights**. Your guide will also tell you about the history of the canyon and the people who have lived there over the ages. You will stop at points of interest and **visit both the Antelope and White House Ruins**, remarkable ancient cliff dwellings. It's best to arrange your guide the night before, but in the slower seasons you can do it the morning of your trip. *Info*: Arrange half-day group guided trips at the Holiday Inn (Tel. 800-465-4329) or Thunderbird Lodge (Tel. 800-679-2473) for $48. Private 3-hour trips are $125 and have to be arranged at the Holiday Inn.

After a quick lunch at the excellent **Thunderbird Lodge cafeteria**, head out to tour the canyon rim on the **South Rim Drive**. Be sure to stop at the **White House Overlook** where you can see the

ALTERNATIVE PLAN: If you don't feel like covering so much territory, plan on spending the entire day at Canyon de Chelly. You can either take a full-day tour or add on the North Rim Drive.

White House cliff dwelling built into the rocks on the other side of the canyon. If you want to stretch your legs, there's a trail at the White House Overlook that leads down to the canyon floor. This is a **steep hike with some sheer dropoffs, but well worth it** if you're fit.

Continue along the South Rim Drive to the **Spider Rock Overlook** at the end of the drive. Be sure to walk to the end of the overlook for a **magical view of Spider Rock** standing 830 feet tall at a junction in the canyon floor. The colors of the canyon walls are spectacular from here as well.

After touring the south rim, you'll make the 2.5-hour drive to spend your evening admiring the **surreal sandstone formations** of the **Monument Valley Navajo Tribal Park**. The valley has been made famous throughout the world because many movies, TV programs, and car commercials have been filmed here. If you arrive before the park closes, take the 17-mile self-guided **Valley Drive**, which passes most of the major formations at 11 marked stops. *Info*: Tel. 435-727-5875. www.navajonationparks.org. Open daily 6am-8pm (May-September) or 8am-5pm (October-April.) $5 age 10 and over.

Finish up at the **Stagecoach Dining Room** at **Goulding's Lodge**. The lodge, technically in Utah but very much a part of the Monument Valley environs, shows off wonderful looks out at the valley. Sitting in front of the view windows eating Navajo-influenced dishes will be a great capper to your evening. *Info*: Tel. 435-727-3231. www.gouldings.com.

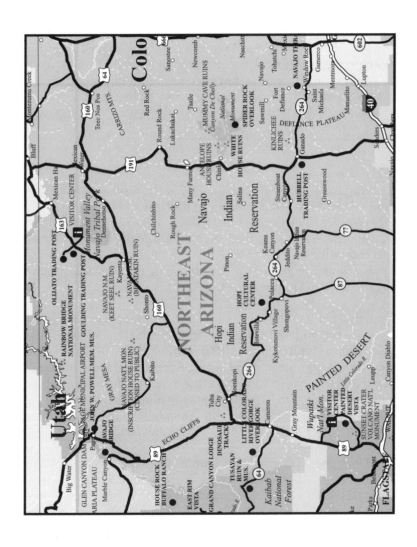

A FANTASTIC WEEKEND IN NORTHEASTERN ARIZONA

With a weekend you can spend a little more time at both **Canyon del Chelly** and **Monument Valley**, as well as add on the incredible ruins of the **Navajo National Monument**. You'll immerse yourself in both ancient and present-day Navajo culture while admiring some of the most memorable rock formations in the state.

Friday Evening

Arriving to impressive **Canyon de Chelly**, head straight to the **South Rim Drive**. If it is winter and the light is fading, go directly to the **Spider Rock Overlook** at the end of the route. Walk all the way out the overlook so that you can admire the wonderful **830-foot monolith** that is Spider Rock. Situated at a junction in the canyon floor, Spider Rock seems to soar against the background of incredible red and orange smooth cliff walls.

From there, if it is still light, stop at the **White House Overlook**. From the rim you can look across the canyon at the White House Ruins, a **preserved 60-room cliff dwelling**. If you've got time and your fitness permits it, there is a wonderful trail here that leads down to the canyon floor. This is the only trail that you can hike without a guide. You'll **follow the path along sheer walls** at the top, so if you are afraid of heights you might want to pass. Make sure you've got time to get back up before dark!

Head to dinner at **Garcia's Restaurant** at what was once Garcia's Trading Post just outside the park entrance in Chinle. (It is now a Holiday Inn but has retained much of its charm.) The home-made bread is quite good although you'll have to ask for more kick in the southwestern dishes if you like spicy food. *Info*: Tel. 800-315-2621. One half mile outside the entrance to Canyon del Chelly: Indian Route 7 - Garcia Trading Post.

Saturday

Even if you didn't spend the night at the **Thunderbird Lodge**, you should head to its excellent cafeteria at the park's entrance for breakfast. After filling up on fry bread and eggs, you'll be ready to enter the canyon for a **half-day tour**. Although you can take your own 4x4 vehicle with a Navajo guide, it's just much nicer to **hire a jeep or join one of the tours**. Your guide will not only drive for you, but also tell you about the history of the canyon and the people who have lived there over the ages.

The canyon itself is remarkable. Smooth red walls soar up 1,000 feet at some places, while cottonwoods grow along side plots of land that have been used by the Navajo people for ages. Your guide will stop at various points of interest and give you time to admire **both the Antelope and White House Ruins**, remarkable ancient cliff dwellings. It's best to arrange your guide the night before, but in the slower seasons you can do it the morning of your trip. *Info*: Arrange half-day group guided trips at the Holiday Inn or Thunderbird Lodge for $48. Private 3-hour trips are $125 and must be arranged at the Holiday Inn. Call 800-679-2473 for reservations.

After your tour, if it's summer, you'll have time to travel the **North Rim Drive**, which extends along the Canyon del Muerto arm of the park. If it's winter, immediately start on the 2.5-hour trip to **Monument Valley Navajo Tribal Park**.

Arriving to Monument Valley, large **buttes, mesas, and canyons** will attract your attention along with unusual **freestanding rock formations**. Some of these amazing sandstone monoliths rise to heights of 1,000 feet above the valley. Stop at the visitor's center and then take the 17-mile self-guided **Valley Drive**, which passes most of the major formations at 11 marked stops. It's definitely worth getting out of the car to go on the **walk from North Window to Cly Butte**. *Info*: Tel. 435-727-5875. www.navajonationparks.org. Open daily 6am-8pm (May-September) or 8am-5pm (October-April.) $5 age 10 and over.

There's really only one choice for dinner near the park, the **Stagecoach Dining Room** at **Goulding's Lodge**. Although

Goulding's is actually located in Utah, it is very much a part of the Monument Valley environs. Grab a seat in front of the view windows and enjoy Navajo-influenced dishes. *Info*: Tel. 435-727-3231. www.gouldings.com.

Sunday

After breakfast at Goulding's, head out on the one-hour drive to the impressive and stunningly beautiful **Navajo National Monument**. Three pueblo ruins dating from the 13th century are preserved beneath enormous cliffs. Two of the ruins, **Betatakin** and **Keet Seel** can visited by **ranger-conducted tours**. Both involve strenuous walks of five and 16 miles respectively. The tours are at different times depending on demand and the season, so **call a few days before you plan to visit**.

Betatakin, which means House on the Ledge, is sheltered in a vast cave in the cliff. It's almost as if a **futuristic dome** has been built over a strange city. It is so remarkable that it is probably **my favorite ruin in Arizona**. The hike takes you down to the amazingly preserved site, which you are allowed to walk through with your guide. You can also **see Betatakin without taking the hike** by following a paved pathway from the visitor's center to an overlook that provides an excellent view of the ruin. *Info*: Tel. 928-672-2700. www.nps.gov/nava/index.htm. Free entry.

ALTERNATIVE PLAN: If you want to **stay and enjoy Monument Valley**, both **horseback and jeep tours** are available into parts of the park that can only be visited with a guide. Make arrangements at Goulding's or in the parking lot at the visitor's center. If you want to **hike on your own**, the wonderfully scenic 3.3 mile Wildcat Trail leaves from the visitor's center and wraps around the West Mitten Butte.

After your hike you can either head **south towards Flagstaff and the Grand Canyon**, stopping at the Cameron Trading Post for dinner (see the Grand Canyon chapter) **or make your way west to Lake Powell** and the **Glen Canyon National Recreation Area**.

A WONDERFUL WEEK IN NORTHEASTERN ARIZONA

You'll have time to cover plenty of ground with a week in this stunning section of the state. You'll learn about native cultures as well as appreciate the fantastic beauty of the national monuments and parks.

RECOMMENDED PLAN: From Flagstaff head north to the Hopi Mesas. Spend a night at the Hopi Cultural Center before moving on to two nights at Canyon de Chelly. Another two nights at Monument Valley will allow you to see everything at a relaxed pace before moving on to Lake Powell for the last days of your week.

Hopi Mesas

The **Hopi Reservation**, completely surrounded by the Navajo Nation and off of the main roads, receives fewer visits from tourists than does the Navajo Nation. If you are interested in learning more about Native American cultures, there is quite a lot to see here. The Hopi, who claim to be descendants of the Anasazi, have lived in the area since the 12th century. Most of the Hopi villages are concentrated on three mesas off of AZ-264. Each of the villages is known for making certain Hopi crafts. Keep in mind that **no photography is allowed** on the Hopi Reservation and that some

Don't Miss...

- **Hopi Mesas** – Walpi on the First Mesa
- **Canyon de Chelly** – South Rim Drive; Canyon Tour
- **Monument Valley** – Valley Drive; hike or horseback ride
- **Navajo National Monument** – Betatakin Ruin
- **Lake Powell** (Glen Canyon National Recreation Area) – Rainbow Bridge; Antelope Canyon

villages are off limits to visitors on certain days of the year.

First Mesa

Known for **pottery and katsina dolls**, the villages of the First Mesa merit a visit for the one-hour **walking tour** offered here. Situated on the edge of steep cliffs with amazing views beyond, the village of **Walpi**, at the end of the tour, is sure to be a highlight of your trip. Tours usually leave Ponsi Hall in Sichomovi 9:30am–5pm daily in summer and 10am-3pm daily the rest of the year. It's best to call ahead however to double check the schedule. *Info*: Tel. 928-737-2262. Off-AZ 264 just past milepost 392: First Mesa Village. $8 adult, $5 children 6–17.

Second Mesa

Besides presenting an opportunity to shop for Hopi crafts, there is an excellent museum here. The **Hopi Cultural Center** has an outstanding collection of **all kinds of Hopi crafts**. You'll also learn about the ancestral spirits that play such an important role in Hopi life. *Info*: Tel 928-734-6650. Highway AZ-264. Open 8am-5pm weekdays and 9am-3pm on weekends. $3 Adults. $1 children under 13.

Hopi Culinary Treats!

If you're not going to spend the night here, you should plan to fill your belly and your tank at the **Hopi Cultural Center** (Tel. 928-734-2401). The restaurant offers you a **chance to sample Hopi dishes**, like blue-corn pancakes. If you are going to spend the night here, make your reservations well in advance.

Third Mesa

The villages of the Third Mesa are known for their weavings of both cloth and baskets. **Stop at Kykotsmovi to get permits to visit the rest of the villages** on the mesa, including Oraibi, what may be the oldest continually inhabited village in the US.

The Navajo Nation

The Navajo Nation, which extends from Arizona into Utah and Nevada, covers 27,000 square miles. Within its borders are an amazing number of national monuments, historical sites, and tribal parks that merit visits.

Hubbell Trading Post National Historic Site

John Hubbell established the post in 1878, and he soon became one of the foremost Indian traders in the American southwest. You can stop by the visitor center as well as **tour the Hubbell home**, which looks much as it did at the time it was acquired by the Hubbell family. Native American's display and sell their crafts and **weaving demonstrations** are given. It is interesting to note that the trading post still serves the same purpose today as it did in the last century. *Info*: Tel. 928-755-3475. Open daily 8am-5pm (6pm in summer.) Free admission.

Window Rock

The **capital of the Navajo Nation**, this side trip is worth a couple of hours if you are interested in Navajo culture because of the **Navajo Tribal Museum** located here. The museum offers a complete history of the Navajo people as well as the natural history of the Four Corners region. *Info*: Tel. 928-871-6544. 8am-6pm daily except Sunday.

The city is named for an impressive round hole ("window") in the sandstone above the city. At the base of the Window Rock you'll find the **Tribal Park and Veteran's Memorial** to honor the many Navajos who served in the U.S. military. Especially important

Four States at Once

Even thought it's kind of silly, plenty of people (including your author) drive out of their way to the Four Corners Monument, where Arizona, New Mexico, Colorado, and Utah meet. You can stand on the brass marker and be in all four states at the same time. There is also a Navajo crafts market there. *Info*: 8am-5pm daily. (7am-7pm in summer.) Admission $1.50.

were the **Code Talkers**, who used their native Navajo language to create a code that was never broken by during World War II. *Info*: Open daily 8am-5pm. Admission free.

Canyon de Chelly National Monument
Located about two miles east of the town of **Chinle**, Canyon de Chelly is one of the highlights of the Navajo Nation. The canyon, although not as deep as the Grand Canyon, is special for both its beauty and historical importance. The **sheer red sandstone walls** of the canyon, ranging from 30 to more than 1,000 feet in height, create a spectacular backdrop for **hundreds of Anasazi ruins**, as well as **present-day Navajo farms**. You can get information about guides and the canyon at the **Visitors Center**, which is open daily from 8am-5pm (6pm in summer.) Horseback and hiking tours can also be arranged.

You must have a guide to enter the canyon, which you can do on either a full or a half-day tour. Although you can take your own 4x4 vehicle, I really **recommend hiring a jeep or joining one of the tours**. That way you can just sit back and take in the amazing contrast of the **red walls and the verdant valley**. Your guide will not only drive for you, but also tell you about the history of the canyon and the people who have lived there over the ages.

The canyon itself is remarkable. Smooth red walls soar up 1,000 feet at some places, while cottonwoods grow along side plots of land that have been used by the Navajo people for years. Your guide will stop at various points of interest and give you time to admire **both the Antelope and White House Ruins**, remarkable ancient cliff dwellings. It's best to arrange your guide the night before, but in the slower seasons you can do it the morning of your trip. *Info*: Arrange group guided trips at the Holiday Inn or Thunderbird Lodge for $48. Private 3-hour trips are $125 and must be arranged at the Holiday Inn. Call 800-679-2473 for reservations.

On the Rim

This is a drive along both the South and North Rims. Each is about 25 miles one way. If you only have time for one, take the South Rim drive because it has the best overlooks. The **North Rim Drive** extends along the Canyon del Muerto arm of the park and has four overlooks.

On the **South Rim Drive**, be sure to stop at the **White House Overlook** where you can see the White House cliff dwelling built into the rocks on the other side of the canyon. There's a great trail at the White House Overlook that leads down to the canyon floor. This is a **steep hike with some sheer drop-offs, but well worth it** if you're fit. Continue along the South Rim Drive to the **Spider Rock Overlook** at the end of the drive. Be sure to walk to the end of the overlook for a **magical view of Spider Rock** standing 830 feet tall at a junction in the canyon floor. The colors of the canyon walls are spectacular from here as well.

Monument Valley Navajo Tribal Park

If you've ever watched a movie, TV, or a car commercial, you'll recognize the unique images of Monument Valley as soon as you arrive. The large **buttes, mesas, and canyons** compete for your attention with unusual **freestanding rock formations**. Some of them can be best described by simply stating their names – The Mittens, Elephant Butte, the Three Sisters, and The Thumb for example. A few of these amazing sandstone monoliths rise to heights of 1,000 feet above the valley.

Stop first at the visitor's center and then take the 17-mile self-guided **Valley Drive**, which passes most of the major formations at 11 marked stops. It's definitely worth getting out of the car to go on the **walk from North Window to Cly Butte**. Both **horseback and jeep tours** are available into

Shop & Eat at Goulding's!

Just across the road from Monument Valley, Goulding's Lodge and Trading Post is a great place to stop for a meal, to shop, or to visit their museum. Learn how the Gouldings brought director John Ford to the area to see the landscape in 1939 and made movie history. It's also a wonderful place to stay. See *Northeasten Sleeps & Eats*.

parts of the park that can only be visited with a guide. Make arrangements in the parking lot at the visitor's center. If you want to **hike on your own**, the Wildcat Trail is phenomenal. The 3.3 mile path leaves from near the visitor's center and wraps around West Mitten Butte. *Info*: Tel. 435-727-5875. www.navajonationparks.org. Open daily 6am-8pm (May-September) or 8am-5pm (October-April.) $5 age 10 and over.

Navajo National Monument

Impressive and stunningly beautiful, the Navajo National Monument protects three pueblo ruins dating from the 13th century. Preserved beneath enormous cliffs, the ruins are in pristine condition. Two of them, **Betatakin** and **Keet Seel** can visited by **ranger-conducted tours**. Both involve strenuous walks of five and 16 miles respectively. The tours are at different times depending on demand and the season, so call a few days before you plan to visit.

Betatakin, which means House on the Ledge, is sheltered in a vast cave in the cliff. It's almost as if a **futuristic dome** has been built over a strange city. It is so remarkable that it is probably **my favorite ruin in Arizona**. The hike takes you down to the remarkably preserved ruin, which you are allowed to walk through with your guide. You can also **see Betatakin without taking the hike** by following a paved pathway from the visitor's center to an overlook that provides an excellent view of the ruin. *Info*: Tel. 928-672-2700. www.nps.gov/nava/index.htm. Free entry.

Lake Powell & Glen Canyon National Recreation Area

Lake Powell, which was created by the construction of the Glen Canyon Dam, is a thing of beauty. Shining a deep blue in the almost guaranteed brilliant sunshine, the lake is 186 miles long and surrounded by towering red sandstone cliffs. Dozens of side canyons, some small and some quite large, add to its mystery for boaters. In the distance is 10,388-foot high Navajo Mountain. The town of **Page** is the headquarters of the vast Glen Canyon National Recreation Area on and around Lake Powell. Page didn't exist until 1956 when construction of a great dam on the Colorado River began.

Visitor Centers

Make at stop at the **Glen Canyon Dam Visitor Center** nestled on the very edge of the canyon wall between the dam's front face and the bridge over the **Colorado River**. Far less known than the Hoover Dam, the Glen Canyon Dam is equal if not better in terms of both structure and setting. Take in the view from the outdoor observation deck, where the river flows hundreds of feet below you. The dam is 710 feet high and its crest is 1560 feet long. You can also take an elevator down to the base of the dam where you get **extraordinary views of the canyon**. *Info*: Tel. 928-608-6404. Open daily 8am-5pm (7am-7pm in summer). Free admission.

While in Page you can check out the **John Wesley Powell Memorial Museum**. With information on Powell's expeditions through the Grand Canyon as well as displays of Native American artifacts, it's an interesting stop. The museum is also a **visitor information center** where you can book different boat and land tours. *Info*: www.powellmuseum.org. Tel. 928-645-9496. Corner of Lake Powell Blvd and Navajo Dr.: 6 North Lake Powell Blvd. 9am-5pm daily. $5 adults. $1 children 5-12.

Lake& Lakeside Attractions

While a small portion of the lake and the encompassing scenery is visible from land, **the only good way to see the area is by boat**, since few roads penetrate any portion of the Glen Canyon Na to tional Recreation Area. I recommend that you take one of the **boat tours offered at the Lake Powell (Wahweap) Marina**. (There are public boat ramps here too if you arrive with your own vessel.) Boat trips vary from as short as an hour to all day. Probably the most popular is the all-day tour to **Rainbow Bridge National Monument**. This incredible sight is the largest known natural bridge in the world. With a height of 270 feet, the bridge really has to be

Rent a Houseboat

Some people swear that the very best way to enjoy Lake Powell is by houseboat. You can explore to your heart's content, move around as you choose, and even sleep under the stars on the deck of the boat if you don't like your quarters below. *Info*: www.lakepowell.com. Tel. 800-528-6154.

seen to be appreciated. Depending on lake levels, you may have to hike about a mile to get to the Rainbow Bridge once you dock. Other tours go to **Antelope and Navajo Canyons** or just around the bay. *Info*: Tel. 800-528-6154. www.lakepowell.com. Prices vary from $50 to $115 for the different cruises.

Antelope Canyon's narrow, red slot ravines, with their **rays of sunlight streaming down**, are almost an iconic image of Arizona. Photographers flock here, but even if you aren't interested in pictures, it's worth a visit because the scenery is amazing. The upper canyon is easy to access – your guide will just drive right up. For this reason it is more crowded than the lower section of the canyon. The lower canyon, which requires using ladders to access, is for the more adventurous. Either way **you have to go with a guide** because it is on Navajo land. *Info*: Lake Powell Jeep Tours, Tel. 928-645-5501. www.blackrabbit.com/antelope.htm. 108 Lake Powell Blvd. in Page.

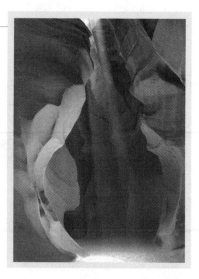

8. EASTERN ARIZONA

The geography of Eastern Arizona ranges from colorful desert landscapes to alpine forests. The northern portion of the region boasts both the Painted Desert and the historic Route 66, and railroad towns of Winslow and Holbrook. Making your way south you'll come to the less-visited but lush and verdant Apache-Sitgreaves National Forest.

Outdoors lovers are in heaven here as the area has miles of hiking and biking trails, excellent trout stream and lakes, reliable snow skiing, and the nation's only designated "primitive area" where no mechanized transportation, including bikes, is allowed. The pleasant hamlet of Greer is located in the real heart of the region, but recreation opportunities also exist to the west in Pinetop-Lakeside and Payson.

ONE GREAT DAY IN EASTERN ARIZONA

Your day will include the amazing natural colors of the Petrified Forest National Park, along with the stepping-into-the-past sensation of visits to Holbrook and Winslow. Add in a charming historic inn with a five-star restaurant and you've got the makings for a wonderful day.

Start your morning off I-40 at the northern entrance to **Petrified Forest National Park,** one of Arizona's most unique attractions. Once part of a gigantic flood plain, tall trees in this area fell and were covered by silt and mud. Over the years, mineral deposits in the ground water seeped into the logs and crystallized, **turning the trees into brightly colored petrified wood.** The same minerals that were responsible for the petrifaction process also resulted in the **incredible colors of the Painted Desert** in the northern part of the park.

Follow the 29-mile park road from north to south. There are a number of excellent overlooks on the first curving section of road. All eight stops along the rim top provide sweeping and ever-changing views of the Painted Desert. If you like to get out and walk, take the easy one-mile **Painted Desert Rim Trail between Tawa and Kachina Points.**

Continue along to the **Newspaper Rock Overlook,** which looks down on a huge **sandstone rock covered with petroglyphs.** Next come the badlands-type **striated formations** known as the **Te-pees.** There are numerous other overlooks and short hikes. Don't miss the easy trails through the colorful petrified wood at the

Crystal Forest and the huge specimens at **Giant Logs.** The **Agate House Trail** is also quite interesting. *Info*: Off I-40 at exit 311. Tel. 928-524-6228. www.nps.gov/pefo. Open 8am-5pm daily. (7am-7pm in summer) $10 per vehicle.

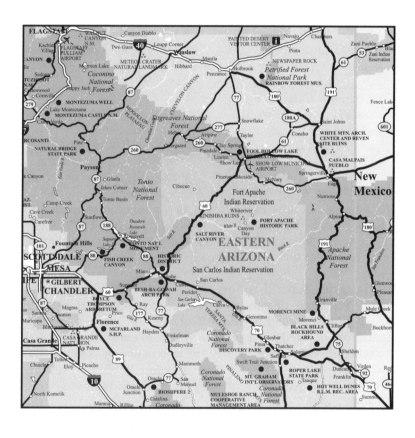

Leave it Alone!

While it is very tempting to pick up a piece of petrified wood and slip it in your pocket, you really shouldn't do it. Not only is it against the law, it is also bad luck! (Check out the letters at the visitor centers from those who took wood home with them and suffered terrible fates.) There are many places in Holbrook that legally sell petrified wood coming from outside the park.

Continue on to **Holbrook**, where you'll swear that the **Route 66 heydays** are still in full swing. The "Main Street of America" runs right through town, and most of the establishments along the route still have their kitschy 1950s look. Stop for lunch at the classic **Joe & Aggie's Mexican Café** (120 W. Hope Dr., Tel. 928-524-6450).

After lunch make your way 33 miles west on I-40 to the **Homolovi Ruins State Park**. A major archeological site dating from the 14th century, these pueblos were **occupied by the ancestors of the modern day Hopi**. Learn about the Homolovi at the visitor center and then go outside to tours the pueblos. *Info*: Off I-40 at Exit 257. Tel. 928-289-4106. www.azstateparks.com/parks/parkhtml/homolovi.html. Open 8am-5pm daily. $5 adults.

End your day at the charming and historic **La Posada Hotel** in nearby **Winslow**. Created to look like a **Spanish hacienda**, La Posada was designed by **Mary Colter**, chief architect and designer for the Fred Harvey Company. Recently restored, this famous railroad hotel is now home to what some consider **the best restaurant in the entire Four Corners Region – the Turquoise Room**. Recreating the elegant dining experience of the Turquoise Room dining car on the Santa Fe's Super Chief, the restaurant offers fantastic fare in a wonderful setting. Start with the **Route 66 Cadillac Margarita** and all will be well in the world. *Info*: Tel 928-289-4366. 303 E. Second Street (Route 66). Open daily breakfast, lunch, and dinner. Dinner reservations recommended.

A FANTASTIC WEEKEND IN EASTERN ARIZONA

With a weekend you'll be able to explore the mountains and rivers of Eastern Arizona's White Mountains from the picturesque village of Greer.

Friday Evening

You'll spend your weekend in and around the small community of **Greer**, an **outdoor enthusiast's paradise** on the banks of the Little Colorado River. Located in the heart of the White Mountains at an **altitude of 8500 feet**, Greer offers hiking, biking, fishing, horseback riding, hunting and skiing. Or, if all you want to do is **sit and enjoy cool weather** while looking at **aspen, willow, and spruce trees**, Greer fits the bill for that as well.

Head to dinner at the **Rendezvous Diner**, housed in what was once Greer's main post office. It's now a wonderful spot for home-cooking and tasty desserts. Ask about pie specials and be sure to order them *a la mode*.

After dinner walk down to the rustic but comfortable **Molly Butler Lodge Lounge**. With a juke box, pool table, and full bar (plus the requisite animal heads on the walls), it's a great place to pass an evening. There's even live music in the summer.

Saturday

If you've come to Greer for outdoor pursuits, get up early and start your day. With **rolling meadows, heavily treed forests, and gentle mountain slopes**, the land in and around the area's **Apache-Sitgreaves National Forest** is reminiscent of East Coast mountain areas.

Anglers should get out to catch some of the **trophy trout** found in the area's lakes, reservoirs and streams. **Hikers** will want to make tracks on the soft **paths that lead through stands of pine and aspen**. The more adventurous might want to tackle the

 Mount Baldy Trail, which climbs almost all the way to the summit of **11,590-ft Mount Baldy,** Arizona's second highest peak. A shorter, but equally beautiful trail summits **Escudilla Mountain**, the state's third highest pinnacle. There are also opportunities for **horseback riding,** and, in the winter, **downhill and cross-country skiing**.

If you'd rather have a **lazy morning in town,** that's an option as well. There are plenty of **antique stores,** as well as the **quaint Butterfly Lodge Museum** to keep you occupied. The Museum, once the home of a western writer and his artist son, displays artifacts and information about their lives. *Info*: On the left as you enter town. Tel. 928-735-7514. Open 10am-5pm Memorial Day-Labor Day, Thursday -Sunday & Holidays. $2 Adult. $1 Youth 12-17.

After a morning of activity, you'll appreciate lunch at the **373 Grill** at the **Greer Lodge Resort**, overlooking the meandering **Little Colorado River**. Eat outside on one of the decks if weather permits.

You can continue your outdoor activities in the afternoon, or, for a change of pace, take a **scenic drive** through the Alpine Region of the Apache-Sitgreaves National Forest. You'll take a section of Highway 191 known as the **Coronado Trail**. The route is reported to trace the course that Francisco Vasquez de Coronado followed in search of the Golden Seven Cities of Cibola in 1540. The **most scenic stretch is between Alpine and Clifton,** but the entire curving drive along forests, meadows and lakes, will elicit exclamations about the **beauty of the high mountain scenery**. With switchbacks, steep grades, and hairpin turns, the route is not for those inclined to motion sickness.

If you don't have time to make the whole drive, consider remote **Hannagan Meadow** at 9100-feet, a wonderful stopping point.

Surrounded by aspen, spruce, and fir, enjoy **dinner at the Hannagan Meadow Lodge** before turning back towards Greer.

ALTERNATIVE PLAN: Book at night at the **Hannagan Meadow Lodge** so that you can explore this remote and beautiful area at your leisure on Sunday morning.

If you've still got some energy when you get back, the Greer Lodge Resort and Amberian Peaks Lodge often host nighttime activities in the summer and over holidays.

Sunday
Spend your morning exactly how you want, whether than means being on a five-mile hike or on a front porch chair.

In the afternoon, if you are headed back to Phoenix, be sure and stop outside of **Pinetop** at the **Mogollon Rim Overlook**. The short trail ends at the top of a sandstone rock outcrop and affords **outstanding views of the valley** beneath the rim. Then continue on through the colorful and gorgeous **Salt River Canyon** before arriving at the Valley of the Sun.

If Flagstaff is your evening destination, the **Petrified Forest National Park** makes a worthy side-tour for the afternoon.

A WONDERFUL WEEK IN EASTERN ARIZONA

A week in this region will take you from the otherworldly landscapes of the Painted Desert and petrified stone to the lush green forests and rivers of the wonderful White Mountains.

RECOMMENDED PLAN: Spend a day visiting the Petrified Forest National Park, overnighting at the historic La Posada in Winslow. From there take off to remote and beautiful Hannagan Meadow for either outdoor pursuits or relaxing wildlife viewing. Then head on for a few days in less-remote but equally enjoyable Greer. Base yourself in Greer for the rest of the week, or, if you want to move on, spend your last couple of days enjoying the Mogollon Rim around Pinetop or Payson.

Winslow/Holbrook

Be sure to make a stop at the **Petrified Forest National Park**, a unique Arizona attraction. About 225 million years ago, tall trees on what was once a giant flood plain fell and were covered by silt and mud. Mineral deposits in the ground water seeped into the logs and crystallized, **turning the trees into brightly colored petrified wood**. These fallen "trees," now as hard as stone, are scattered across the desert in this National Park.

Don't Miss...

- Petrified Forest National Park
- Turquoise Room at La Posada
- Coronado Trail to Hannagan Meadow
- Hiking, fishing, skiing, or horseback riding in Greer

The 29-mile park road, which runs north-south, can be driven in either direction. I'll take it from north to south for this description. The first part of the drive offers excellent views of the **Painted Desert**. Stop at some or all of the eight overlooks along the rim top to enjoy sweeping and ever-changing views. Take the easy one-mile **Painted Desert Rim Trail between Tawa and Kachina Points** if you like to walk.

The **Newspaper Rock Overlook** is worth a stop as it looks down on a huge sandstone rock covered with **petroglyphs**. Don't miss the easy trails through the colorful petrified wood at the **Crystal Forest** and the huge specimens at **Giant Logs**. The **Agate House Trail** leads to a semi- restored **pueblo constructed entirely of petrified wood**. The **Rainbow Forest Museum** at the southern end of the park is worth a stop if you're interested in **dinosaur skeletons**. *Info*: Off I-40 at exit 311. Tel. 928-524-6228. www.nps.gov/pefo. Open 8am-5pm daily. (7am-7pm in summer) $10 per vehicle.

The southern end of the park is very near the town of **Holbrook**. The "Mother Road," **Route 66**, runs right through town, and most of the establishments along the route have kept the look from their 1950s glory days. If you're in town at meal time, **Joe & Aggie's Mexican Café** (120 W. Hope Dr., Tel. 928-524-6450) offers excellent food with classic Route 66 kitsch.

About 33 miles west of Holbrook is the **Homolovi Ruins State Park**. These pueblos, dating from the 14th century, were **occupied by the ancestors of the modern day Hopi**. This is a sacred site to them, so tread with respect. You can learn about the Homolovi at the visitor center and then go outside to tours the pueblos. *Info*: Off I-40 at Exit 257. Tel. 928-289-4106. www.azstateparks.com/parks/parkhtml/homolovi.html. Open 8am-5pm daily. $5 adults.

The White Mountains

Generally contiguous with the **Apache-Sitgreaves National Forest**, the White Mountains are unusual in Arizona. These **heavily forested mountains** appear more like the mountains of the East Coast than the usually arid looking western peaks. There are also a **large number of natural lakes**. With elevations generally in the five to six-thousand-foot level, the weather is cooler and there is more rainfall than in other parts of the state. The result is a **vast oasis and popular playground** for Phoenix residents. Outside of Arizona the area is not well known at all, but it merits a visit if you've got the time.

In the sister cities of **Springerville and Edgar**, you'll have a chance to visit the **Casa Malpais Pueblo**. There is a

Stay at La Posada

If you're going to be in the area in the evening, end your day at the charming and historic La Posada Hotel in nearby Winslow. This famous railroad hotel is home the Turquoise Room, one of the best restaurants in the region (see *Winslow Sleeps & Eats*).

Frontier Women

Across from the Springerville post office on Main Street you'll see the Madonna of the Trail, one of 12 statues built in the 1930s in various parts of the country to honor the spirit of America's pioneer women. Clothed in frontier dress and a large sunbonnet, the statue holds both a rifle and an infant, which seems to be the ultimate in multi-tasking.

museum onsite with displays about the Mogollon Indian culture. Guided tours of the 15-acre ruin site are offered as well. The pueblo, built around 1250, contains the **main pueblo with more than 100 rooms** and the Great Kiva. *Info*: 318 Main St. in Springerville. Tel. 928-333-5375. 8am-5pm (4pm Friday-Sunday). Tours at 9am, 11am, and 2pm. Tour $5 adults.

Continue south on the section of Highway 191 known as the **Coronado Trail**. The route is reported to trace the course that Francisco Vasquez de Coronado followed in search of the Golden Seven Cities of Cibola in 1540. Enjoy the curving drive along forests, meadows and lakes that highlights the **beauty of the high mountain scenery**. The route officially runs all the way to Clifton, but you can stop at Hannagan Meadow for a few days of R&R.

The remote **Hannagan Meadow**, elevation 9100-feet, is a wonderful stopping point for a few days of outdoor activities on **thousands of acres of beautiful forests and trails**. You can hike, horseback ride, fish, camp, hunt, mountain bike and ski in the area. You might also see a **gray wolf**, as this is site where the endangered species reintroduction program was started in 1997.

Stay, eat, and recreate at the **Hannagan Meadow Lodge** or camp at the Hannagan Campground. You can also access

Don't Skip Out on the Bill!

Pay your bills when you leave. Hannagan Meadow was named for rancher Robert Hannagan who, in the early 1900's, was **chained to a tree until his son paid off his $1200 debt**. You wouldn't want the same to happen to you.

the **Blue Range Primitive Area** from here. The last Primitive Area in the United States, it is off-limits to all motorized and mechanized vehicles – even bicycles! (See *Eastern Arizona Best Activities*.)

Greer, at the end of AZ-373, is another good stopping point for a few days of R&R. An **outdoor enthusiast's paradise** on the banks of the Little Colorado River, Greer offers many of the same activities of Hannagan Meadow, but in a slightly more "civilized" environment. There are lodges and inns that cater to all budgets.

With rolling meadows, heavily treed forests, and gentle mountain slopes, the land around Greer offers numerous active pursuits. **Anglers** rave about the **trophy trout** found in the area's lakes, reservoirs and streams, while **hikers** make tracks on the soft **paths that lead through stands of pine and aspen**. Two wonderful hikes include the 8-mile one-way Mount Baldy Trail, which climbs almost all the way to the summit of **11,590-ft Mount Baldy**, Arizona's second highest peak and the shorter, but equally beautiful trail that summits **Escudilla Mountain**, the state's third highest pinnacle.

There are also plenty of **antique stores**, as well as the **quaint Butterfly Lodge Museum**. The Museum, once the home of a western writer and his artist son, displays artifacts and information about their lives. *Info*: On the left as you enter town. Tel. 928-735-7514. Open 10am-5pm Memorial Day-Labor Day, Thursday -Sunday & Holidays. $2 Adult. $1 Youth 12-17.

In the winter, skiers flock to nearby **Sunrise Park Resort**. Their 65 runs off of ten lifts offer challenges for skiers of all levels, although the majority of the runs are beginner and intermediate. They also have a separate snowboarding area, cross-country ski trails and a special children's "ski-wee" area.

Pinetop-Lakeside
Further west on AZ-260, **Pinetop-Lakeside** is the **largest and most developed recreational center** in the area. The summer population here can reach as high as 30,000 as desert dwellers

from Phoenix seek higher ground. There are many lakes and an **extensive trail system** for hiking and biking. A highlight of this area is the **Mogollon Rim Overlook**, two miles northwest of town. An easy nature trail is marked with signs pointing out the abundant natural resources found in this area. The trail ends at the top of a sandstone rock outcrop with an outstanding view of the valley beneath the rim.

Payson

The scenic drive along AZ-260 from Pinetop to **Payson** roughly parallels the Mogollon Rim. The road passes though a number of towns and recreational areas before a **series of rather steep switchbacks** brings you from the top of the rim into Payson, at the rim's base. Like Pinetop-Lakeside, **Payson is a center for services related to the many recreational pursuits** found in the White Mountains.

A highlight here is the **Tonto Natural Bridge State Park**. Composed of travertine, the bridge is 183 feet high while the space beneath it measures about 150 feet in height and almost 400 feet across. It is one of the largest natural structures of its type in the entire world and is visible from several viewpoints in the park. There is also a trail that leads from the top of bride into the canyon beneath. *Info*: 10 miles north of Payson on AZ-87. Tel. 928-476-4202. 9am-5pm daily (8am-7pm in summer). $5 per vehicle.

9. WESTERN ARIZONA

The western portion of Arizona is a land of wide-open spaces dotted by widely spaced towns. This entire region is almost all high desert, which explains why its most important natural feature is the life-sustaining Colorado River. The river and its dams are the basis for numerous communities along its banks, like Lake Havasu and Bullhead City/ Laughlin, which offer wet recreational pursuits in the middle of the desert.

More centrally located in the region, Kingman provides a glimpse back at the hey-day of "The Mother Road," Route 66. To the east of Kingman you'll find Wickenburg, one of the dude ranch capitals of the state.

ONE GREAT DAY IN WESTERN ARIZONA

You'll start in the historic town of Kingman, with its still-strong ties to Route 66. After poking around town you can either head underground, to Grand Canyon Caverns, or visit the old mining town of Chloride.

Begin your day in the historic downtown area, centered around Beale Street. Walk down Beale to the **Mohave Museum of History and Art**. The museum contains displays and several dioramas that trace the area history, including that of the Mohave and Hualapai Indian tribes. Another section of the museum houses a tribute to television and movie star **Andy Devine** — the most famous person to come out of Kingman. *Info*: Tel. 928-753-3195. Monday-Friday 9am-5pm. Weekends 1pm-5pm. $2 adults. $1 children.

A little further along is the **Bonelli House**. Considered **one of the best examples of the Anglo-territorial architectural style**, it contains many original and period pieces and is typical of the home of a prosperous Kingman family at the turn of the 20th century. A highlight is the large wall clock that, at one time, was the only clock in Kingman. *Info*: 430 E Spring St. Tel. 928-753-3175. Monday-Friday 11am-3pm.

While you're downtown, don't miss the relatively new **Route 66 Museum**. The first paved transcontinental road in the country, Route 66 kept Kingman hopping in the 50s and 60s. Learn all about the importance of the "Mother Road" and see **fun displays such as old diners** and period gas pumps. *Info*: 120 West Andy Devine Ave. in the Powerhouse Visitor's Center. Tel. 928-753-9889. Open 9am-6pm daily.

After lunch, head out US-93 to the **historic mining town of Chloride**. At one time more than 75 separate silver mines supported a population of over 2,000 people. Now there are only about 300 residents, mostly artisans and craftsmen, who have set

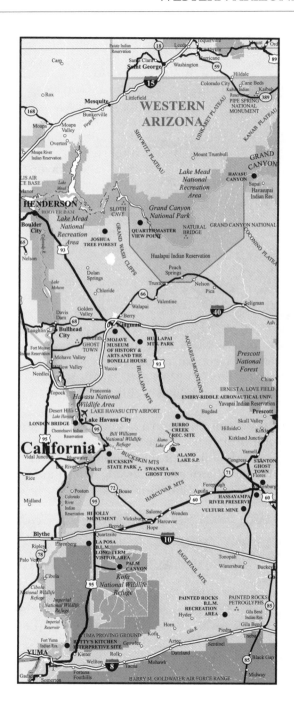

ALTERNATIVE PLAN: The **Hualapai Mountain Park**, south of town, is located at an elevation of 8,400 feet. In the summer this means **relief from the scorching temperatures** of lower terrain. Hike or bike the **extensive trail system** if you prefer an active day in the woods. There are cabins and campgrounds as well if you'd like to spend more time there. *Info:* www.mcparks.com/hmp. Hualapai Mountain Park, 6230 Hualapai Mountain Road. Tel. (877) 757-0915.

up shop in some of the town's historic buildings. It's a great place to go if you're looking for antiques and kids will like visiting the old jail.

If it's a hot summer day, you might enjoy the cool climate of the **Grand Canyon Caverns** in the afternoon. This large cave is filled with **colorful formations and marine fossils** dating back more than three million years. The caverns contain the mummified remains of some animals and evidence of visitation by Native Americans. Guided tours begin with **a 21-story elevator descent** into the cool 56-degree cavern. The tour, on well-lit paved trails, lasts about 45 minutes. *Info:* East of Kingman on AZ-66. Tel. 928-422-3223. 10am-4pm daily (8am-6pm in summer.) $13 adults. $10 children 4-12.

After your afternoon trip, return to downtown Kingman to the historic **Hotel Brunswick.** Built in 1909, the hotel was once the only three-story building for miles around. Dine at the hotel's delightful **Hubb's Bistro** before turning in for the evening. (315 East Andy Devine. Tel. 928-718-1800.)

A FANSTASTIC WEEKEND IN WESTERN ARIZONA

With a weekend in Western Arizona you can enjoy one of the wonderful dude ranches around Wickenburg. Whether you want to learn to rope cattle, or prefer to ride in the morning and hit the links in the afternoon, there's a guest ranch to meet every need.

Because most of the ranches follow their own weekend schedules, you'll have to find some time to visit the **Desert Caballeros
Western Museum** in **Wickenburg** on your way in or out of town.
In addition to rotating special exhibits, the permanent collection
includes a fine Western art exhibit featuring such famous American artists as Frederick Remington and Robert Daughters. There
is an excellent Native American gallery as well. Authentic western and native items are on sale at the museum's store. *Info*: 21
North Frontier St. Tel. 928-684-2272. 10am-5pm daily. (12pm-
4pm Sunday.) $5 adults. $1 children 6-16.

Rancho de los Caballeros, is one of the **largest and most luxurious guest ranches** in Arizona. A historic property covering some
20,000 acres of mountain the desert scenery, the ranch has a golf
club and swimming pool among its many amenities. Non-riders
can enjoy the nature program, bird watching, or even a massage.
Cookouts and evening entertainment make for enjoyable evenings. There is also a good children's program. *Info*: 1551 S.
Vulture Mine Road. Tel. 800-684-5030. www.sunc.com. 77 rooms.
Open October-May.

Kay El Bar Guest Ranch, built in 1926, features authentic adobe-
style buildings that **house only 24 guests** at one time. This makes
for an informal and intimate atmosphere. No more than six riders
are on any one ride. You'll definitely feel like part of the family
here. The homey lodge living room often features western entertainers at night for singing and cowboy poetry. Wonderful meals
cooked from scratch. *Info*: Just past mile marker 198 on US-89 out
of Wickenburg. Tel. 800-684-7583. www.kayelbar.com. 8 rooms
and 4 houses.

Flying E Ranch, with only
16 rooms, offers personalized vacations on a 20,000-
acre working ranch. Situated
on the outskirts of
Wickenburg in the shadow
of Vulture Peak, the ranch
traverses picturesque desert
scenery. Other amenities

include a pool and tennis court. *Info*: 2801 W. Wickenburg Way. Tel. 928-684-2690. www.flyingeranch.com. 14 rooms. 3 suites.

A WONDERFUL WEEK IN WESTERN ARIZONA

With a week in Western Arizona you can see impressive natural and man-made wonders, spend some time enjoying the lakes created by damming the Colorado River, and then experience real cowboy life at a dude ranch.

RECOMMENDED PLAN: Start in Kingman and take a couple of days exploring both the town and the surrounding area, including Hoover Dam. From there head south to Lake Havasu's London Bridge for a day or two. After that, finish up your week at one of Wickenburg's guest ranches for a real taste of the west.

Kingman
Tracing its beginnings to the coming of the railroad in 1880, Kingman is sustained by its important location on the interstate and its historic location on Route 66. The historic downtown area is centered around Beale Street. Start at the **Mohave Museum of History and Art**. The museum contains displays and several dioramas that trace the area history, including that of the Mohave and Hualapai Indian tribes. The most famous person to come out of Kingman is **movie star Andy Devine**. Another section of the museum houses a tribute to his television and movie star days. *Info*: Tel. 928-753-3195. Monday-Friday 9am-5pm. Weekends 1pm-5pm. $2 adults. $1 children.

Associated with and just down the street from the museum is the **Bonelli House**. Considered **one of the best examples of the Anglo-territorial architectural style**, it contains period pieces typical of a home of a prosperous Kingman family at the turn of the 20th century. A highlight is the large wall clock that, at one time, was the only clock in Kingman. *Info*: 430 E Spring St. Tel. 928-753-3175. Monday-Friday 11am-3pm.

Another good downtown stop is the relatively new **Route 66 Museum**. The first paved transcontinental road in the country, Route 66 kept Kingman hopping in the 50s and 60s. The exhibits include **old diners and period gas pumps**. *Info*: 120 West Andy Devine Ave. in the Powerhouse Visitor's Center. Tel. 928-753-9889. Open 9am-6pm daily.

Don't Miss...

• **Historic Kingman** with its Route 66 past
• **Lake Havasu** and the real London Bridge
• A **trail ride** at one of Wickenburg's guest ranches

If you're in Kingman at mealtime, or if you just want a cool drink, stop by the historic **Hotel Brunswick** for a refreshing step back in time. Built in 1909, the hotel was once the only three-story building for miles around. (315 East Andy Devine. Tel. 928-718-1800.)

Around Kingman

The **old mining town of Chloride** is a delightful day trip from Kingman. At one time more than 75 separate silver mines supported a population of over 2,000 people. Now the 300 residents, mostly artisans and craftsmen, have set up shop in some of the town's historic buildings. It's a fun place to spend a while poking around antique shops and galleries.

Continuing north, you'll reach the **Hoover Dam**, one of the great engineering wonders of the world. Seven hundred twenty six feet high, and completed in 1935, the dam is **best visited early in the day** before the throngs arrive from nearby Las Vegas. Several parking areas on the Arizona side provide a **panoramic view** of the top of the dam, with the brilliant azure blue of Lake Mead behind it and the dark Colorado River below. You can walk across to the Nevada side of the dam, where the visitor's center is located, for tours and more information. *Info*: US93. Tel. 702-494-2517. 9am-6pm daily. $7 for visitor's center parking. Tours $11 adults, $6 children 7-16.

Another sight north of Kingman is a **remote section of the Grand Canyon**, known as **Grand Canyon West**. It is actually more easily accessed from Kingman than from the South Rim of the canyon. (See the Grand Canyon chapter for more details on Grand Canyon West.)

East of Kingman you'll find the delightfully cool **Grand Canyon Caverns**. You can see **colorful formations and marine fossils** dating back more than three million years as well as evidence of visitation by Native Americans. Guided tours begin with **a 21-story elevator descent** into the 56-degree cavern. The tour, on well-lit paved trails, lasts about 45 minutes. *Info*: East of Kingman on AZ-66. Tel. 928-422-3223. 10am-4pm daily (8am-6pm in summer.) $13 adults. $10 children 4-12.

The most popular spot west of Kingman is **Bullhead City**, with the **casinos of Laughlin, Nevada** on the other side of the river. Despite its rather isolated location Laughlin receives several million visitors a year, mostly residents of California or Arizona who come to gamble. Regular water taxi service connects Bullhead City to the **hotel-casinos lined up along the banks of the Nevada side of the Colorado River**. Most of the casinos are "branches" of those in Vegas. If you have some itchy fingers that want to part with some bucks, give gaming in Laughlin a try.

Hikers and bikers will want to travel just south of Kingman to the **Hualapai Mountain Park**. With an **elevation of 8400 feet**, the

park is cool and even forested in some sections. There is an **extensive trail system** where you might spot deer and elk as you hike. You can even rent a picnic kit, with a volleyball and net, softball bats, balls and bases, a soccer ball and horseshoes. *Info*: Hualapai Mountain Park, 6230 Hualapai Mountain Road. Tel. (877) 757-0915. www.mcparks.com/hmp.

Lake Havasu City

One of Arizona's popular "west coast" resort destinations, Lake Havasu City sits on the east side of the lake of the same name. It's a beautiful **lake destination**, but the real highlight is the **famous London Bridge**. The London Bridge survived many historic events in England, but could not withstand nature's sinking forces. In 1968, the city of London decided to sell the sinking bridge for 2.5 million dollars to Robert P. McCulloch, founder of Lake Havasu City. **Transported brick-by-brick** from its original Thames River location, the bridge was rebuilt across a small man-made channel of the Colorado River. The bridge is open at all times and illuminated at night. An "English village" has grown up around the bridge, offering shopping and restaurants in Tudor-style buildings. It's a bit cheesy, but if you get in the mood and just go with the theme, it can be fun.

The surrounding resort area covers 110 acres and features **all sorts of recreation opportunities**, lake cruises, and a marina. You can rent any kind of boat or personal watercraft and enjoy the almost always sunny weather. The lake and river can be **seen best by boat tours**. Try Blue Water Jet Boat tours for a two-hour trip up the Colorado River (Tel. 888-855-717. www.coloradoriverjetboattours.com). Western Arizona Canoe & Kayak Outfitters is a good option if you prefer to travel under your own steam. (Tel. 888-881-5038. www.azwacko.com.)

The excellent **Havasu National Wildlife Refuge** is located just to the north, in scenic Topock Gorge. It can be seen by either boat or foot trail. **Geese, egrets, and heron** are big attractions to birders. *Info*: Tel. 760-326-3853. www.fws.gov/southwest/refuges/arizona/havasu. 8am-4pm daily.

Yuma

Despite being **one of the hottest locations in the United States**, it is the weather in Yuma that attracts so many visitors. Comfortable winters, low humidity, and **sunshine a staggering 93% of the time**, make Yuma ideal for every sun worshipper.

Start your day at the **Yuma Territorial Prison State Park**, situated on a high bluff overlooking the Colorado River. A **maximum** security prison from 1876-1909, when Arizona really was the Wild West, it can now be toured on your own or with a guide. Don't miss the solitary confinement area known as "the hole." *Info*: 1 Prison Hill Road. Tel. 928-783-4771. www.azstateparks.com/Parks/parkhtml/yuma.html. 8am-5pm daily. $5 adults. $2 children.

Nearby on 2nd Avenue on a site by the Colorado River that also faces Yuma's city hall is the **Yuma Crossing State Historic Park**. A Quartermaster Depot was established here in 1865 to serve as a major storage and distribution point for supplies. **Guides costumed in period clothing** are on hand to relate the tales and history of the site. Also located here is a Southern Pacific steam locomotive. *Info*: 201 N. 4th Avenue. Tel. 928-329-0471. www.azstateparks.com/Parks/parkhtml/yumacross.html. 9am-5pm daily. $5 adults. $2 children.

Nice Stop in Yuma

Try the Garden Café, behind the Sanguinetti House, for a nice breakfast or lunch in the inviting tree-shaded garden. Leave room for dessert. (250 Madison Ave. Tel. 928-783-1491.)

A final downtown stop is the Sanguinetti **House Museum**. The former home of a wealthy Yuma merchant, the house now exhibits furnishings and artifacts representative of Yuma's frontier period. The original owner had a colorful garden with bird aviaries and these are also maintained as they were in the past. The **talking birds are sure to delight children**. *Info*: 240 Madison Avenue. Tel. 928-782-1841. www.yumalibrary.org/ahs. Tuesday-Saturday 10am-4pm. $3 adults. $2 children 12-18.

Wickenburg

Tracing its origins to prospector Henry Wickenburg, the town of Wickenburg was once an important center for gold, copper and silver mining. It prospers now because of its **great weather and dude ranches**. Visit one of the state's guest ranches if you get the chance. Wickenburg has three that are members of the reputable **Arizona Dude Ranch Association**. Some guest ranches are true working ranches and others are ranch vacation destinations – be sure to decide which you want before you make reservations.

Rancho de los Caballeros, is one of the **largest and most luxurious guest ranches** in Arizona. A historic property covering some 20,000 acres of mountain the desert scenery, the ranch has a golf club and swimming pool among its many amenities. Non-riders can enjoy the nature program, bird watching, or even a massage. Cookouts and evening entertainment make for enjoyable evenings. There is also a good children's program. *Info*: 1551 S. Vulture Mine Road. Tel. 800-684-5030. www.sunc.com. 77 rooms. Open October-May.

Kay El Bar Guest Ranch, built in 1926, features authentic adobe-style buildings that **house only 24 guests** at one time. This makes for an informal and intimate atmosphere. No more than six riders are on any one ride. You'll definitely feel like part of the family here. The delightful lodge living room often features western entertainers at night for singing and cowboy poetry. Wonderful meals cooked from scratch. *Info*: Just past mile marker 198 on US-89 out of Wickenburg. Tel. 800-684-7583. www.kayelbar.com. 8 rooms and 4 houses.

Flying E Ranch, with only 16 rooms, offers personalized vacations on a 20,000-acre working ranch. Situated on the outskirts of Wickenburg in the shadow of Vulture Peak, the ranch traverses picturesque desert scenery. Other amenities include a pool and tennis court. *Info*: www.flyingeranch.com. 2801 W. Wickenburg Way. Tel. 928-684-2690. 14 rooms. 3 suites.

Even if you don't have the time or budget for a guest ranch stay, you can get a taste of the west at the **Desert Caballeros Western Museum**. In addition to rotating special exhibits, the permanent collection includes fine Western art by such famous American artists as Frederick Remington and Charles Russell. There is an excellent Native American gallery as well. Authentic western and native items are on sale at the museum's store. *Info*: 2801 W. Wickenburg Way. Tel. 928-684-2690. www.flyingeranch.com. 14 rooms. 3 suites.

10. ARIZONA IN TWO WEEKS

With two weeks in the state you'll have time to visit the majority of Arizona's fantastic natural wonders. At the same time, you won't be so rushed that you arrive home completely exhausted from your "vacation." Not only will you travel to outstanding physical landscapes, you'll also experience both Native American and Hispanic traditions. Throw in the cultural amenities of the state's largest cities, and you've got the ingredients for a wonderful fortnight.

For each of the destinations here, refer to the maps in chapters 3-9.

RECOMMENDED PLAN: I've paced the itinerary so that you are often able to spend two nights at the same hotel. This is much more relaxing than packing and unpacking every single day and it allows you to get more of a feel for some of the destinations. I also assume that you'll start and finish the loop in Phoenix – that is, you'll fly into Phoenix and then drive to Sedona. You'll spend one night in Sedona, two in Flagstaff, one at the Grand Canyon, two at Lake Powell, one at Monument Valley, two at Canyon de Chelly, one at Hannagan Meadow, two in Tucson, and the last night back in Phoenix.

SEDONA
Renowned for its fantastic red rock formations and mild year-round temperatures, Sedona is a wonderful place to start your tour of the state.

En Route
On your way to Sedona on I-17, don't miss the **cliff dwellings at Montezuma Castle National Monument**. These impressive ruins, located along a pleasant tree-shaded creek, are an excellent example of Sinagua architecture. The five-story dwelling, built into the hollow of an imposing vertical cliff, was constructed in the early 1100s. Definitely worth a stop. *Info*: Exit 289, three

miles off Interstate 17. Tel. 928-567-3322. www.nps.gov/moca/index.htm. Open daily 8am-5pm (6pm in summer). Admission $5 ages 16 and over.

In Town
One of the best ways to experience the red rocks of Sedona is to **hike among the formations**. A nice hike can be found at the appropriately named **Bell Rock** on 179 as you approach town. The easy alternative is simply to walk out to the base of Bell Rock, or, for a little more challenge, you can enjoy the mostly-level

Don't Miss...

• Sedona's Red Rock formations
• Wupatki and Sunset Crater National Monuments near Flagstaff
• Peering into the Grand Canyon
• A boat tour on Lake Powell
• The Navajo Nation's Canyon de Chelly and Monument Valley
• The Coronado Trail to Hannagan Meadow in Eastern Arizona
• Tucson's Sonoran Desert Museum and Historic Downtown
• Scottsdale's world-class resorts, shopping, and fine dining
• The famous Heard Museum in Phoenix

five-mile hike around the mesmerizing Bell Rock and Courthouse Buttes. *Info*: 6.4 miles south of the 89/179 "Y" on 179. The trailhead and parking will be on your left. $5 Red Rock Pass required. You can buy passes at the trailhead or any of the Visitor's Centers.

After your hike, stop at the **Chapel of the Holy Cross**. This chapel, impressively situated between two huge red sandstone peaks, offers wonderful panoramic views that will move you no matter your religious leanings. *Info*: Located on Chapel Road off of AZ 179 three miles south of the "Y." Tel. 928-282-4069. Open daily 9am-5pm. No admission fee but donations accepted.

If you prefer more adventure, you can line up a **Jeep Tour** (see *Sedona Best Activities*.) The open-topped jeeps take you up, over, and down what appear to be impossibly steep red rock routes.

If you don't want to hike, you can drive the **Red Rock Loop** west of town on 89A for spectacular views. The route will take you through the magnificent formations of **Red Rock State Park** as well as the impressive hoodoos and spires of Cathedral Rock. *Info*: The paved Red Rock Loop Road is located west of Sedona off of 89A. If you wish to enter Red Rock State Park there is a $5 entry fee.

Originally an artist's colony, Sedona still has a rich cache of art galleries. You can stroll through the **shops and galleries of**

Tlaquepaque as well as enjoy dinner here. Located along Oak Creek under the shade of large sycamore trees, Tlaquepaque is set up to resemble a Mexican pueblo. You'll enjoy the pleasant patios and fountains even if shopping is not your thing.

FLAGSTAFF
A laid-back mountain town, Flagstaff is a popular spot year-round because of cool summer temperatures and winter mountain sports. You'll spend two nights here so that you have time to see both the in and out-of-town attractions.

En Route
Travel from Sedona to Flagstaff via 89A to experience the beauty of **Oak Creek Canyon**. The road slithers through red rock spires up to pine and juniper trees on the edge of the Colorado Plateau. The cliff walls tower as much as a thousand feet above the road in places. Don't miss the **Oak Creek Vista**, an overlook at the top of the canyon with wonderful views as well as a Native American crafts cooperative.

In Town
The **Museum of Northern Arizona** is a good stop to acquaint yourself with the culture of the Colorado Plateau region, where you'll be spending much of the next week. With exhibits that cover anthropology, biology, geology and fine arts, the museum offers something for everybody. *Info*: Three miles north of town on Highway 180 (3101 North Fort Valley Road.) Tel. 928-774-5213. www.musnaz.org. Open daily 9am-5pm. Admission $5 adults; $2 children 7-17.

Just a few miles past the museum you'll find **Arizona Snowbowl**, a year-round **playground for outdoor lovers** and a great place to catch wonderful views. During the summer you can **ride the chair lift** up the mountain to 11,500 feet and see all the way to the Grand Canyon. There are also some wonderful hikes that start near the base of the chairlift (see *Flagstaff Best Activities*). You can even climb Humphrey's Peak, the highest point in Arizona at 12,633 feet. *Info*: Take Highway 180 seven miles north of Flagstaff to Snowbowl Road and continue up the mountain seven miles. Tel. 928-779-1951. www.arizonasnowbowl.com. Costs and hours vary depending on activity.

To get a real feel for Flagstaff, you have to spend a while downtown at **Heritage Square**. There are multiple concerts and events here each week, from movies to salsa dancing and a bit of everything in between. Check out the base of the flagpole, which is made of rock from each of the layers of the Grand Canyon. You can also enjoy the many shops, restaurants and galleries located around the square. *Info*: Downtown on Aspen between San Francisco and Leroux Streets. www.heritagesquaretrust.org.

Architecture and design fans will love the **Riordan Mansion State Historic Park**. The 40-room mansion, built in 1904, is a well-restored example of Arts and Crafts style architecture. The guided one-hour tour takes you through many of the rooms, all of which are decorated with original furnishings. You learn much about the history of Flagstaff as well. It might sound kind of boring, but it's really quite fascinating. *Info*: Half a mile north of the intersection of I-17 and I-40 at 1300 Riordan Ranch St. Tel. 928-779-4395. www.azstateparks.com/Parks/parkhtml/riordan.html. 10:30am-5:30pm daily (8:30am in summer.) $5 adults. $2.50 children under 17.

Both budding and wannabe astronomers will enjoy the **Lowell Observatory**, famous for discovering the planet Pluto. Daytime tours feature astronomy exhibits and a walk through the facilities, while nighttime visitors get to observe the night sky through telescopes. *Info*: 1400 West Mars Hill Road. Tel. 928-774-3358. www.lowell.edu. Open for both day and evening tours. Extended summer hours. Admission $5 adults. $2 children 5-17.

Near Town
It's worth another day in Flagstaff to explore the national monuments located very nearby. Take US-89 twelve miles north of town and follow the signs to **Sunset Crater Volcano National Monument**, the site of a massive volcanic eruption and extensive

lava flow over 900 years ago. The self-guide hike along the **Bonito Lava Flow Trail** leads through a fascinating array of volcanic formations and is well-worth your time.

From there continue along the loop road to the **Wupatki National Monument**, partially restored ruins from native Anasazi and Sinagua civilizations. Stop at the Visitor's Center to tour the Wupatki ruins, the largest complex in the park. The ruins include an ancient amphitheater as well as a unique ball court. There is also an interesting blow-hole at the end of the trail. *Info*: Off US-89 north of Flagstaff. Tel. 928-679-2365. www.nps.gov/wupa/index.htm. Open daily 9am-5pm. $5 adults 17 and older.

For another look at native cultures, stop at the **Walnut Canyon National Monument** on your way back to Flagstaff. You'll hike down a steep paved trail to visit the remains of a Sinagua community that developed between 1125 and 1250 AD. The dwellings are built beneath overhanging cliffs and are quite interesting. *Info*: 7.5 miles east of Flagstaff on I-40 (exit 204.) Tel. 928-526-3367. www.nps.gov/waca. Open daily 9am-5pm. $5 adults 17 and older.

GRAND CANYON
Continue your trip by traveling to the **South Rim of the Grand Canyon**, only about an hour from Flagstaff. This **majestic natural wonder** will surely be a highlight of your trip. Take off from Flagstaff early in the morning so that you'll have almost two full days at this most impressive Arizona attraction.

En Route
If you'd like to see the **canyon by air**, your flight will leave from outside the park at the **Grand Canyon Airport**. While flights have been restricted due to the noise pollution they cause, there are still many available if you reserve in advance (see Grand Canyon Chapter). If you are not hiking into the canyon, this is a way to see it from another perspective than that of the rim.

At the Canyon
Mather Point is the first overlook as you enter the park from the US180/AZ 64 entrance. As you get your first glimpse over the

 rim, you will be blown away by the sheer scale of the canyon. It is huge and makes everything else seem insignificant in comparison. The next overlook at **Yavapai Point** not only offers a beautiful view, but also a small museum.

The **Grand Canyon village** is next. It is the most crowded part of the park, but that's because the majority of services and hotels are located here as well as the **Visitor Center**. It is also the **departure point for the shuttle** during the summer months when car travel is not allowed along the West Rim drive. Take some time to walk along the rim trail in front of the village. The views get better and better at every turn.

If you are up for the task physically, I highly recommend a **hike part-way into the canyon**. The **Bright Angel Trail**, which starts here at the village, is an excellent option. The trail winds down a series of steep switch-backs to the Colorado River far below. Even if you only go for a few minutes, it's fun to start a descent into the canyon. Never try to go down to the river and back in a single day and be sure to take plenty of water.

After your hike, you won't want to miss the amazing array of colors hitting the canyon at sunset. **Hopi and Pima points on the West Rim are prime sunset-watching spots**. Dinner at the **El Tovar Dining Room** in the historic El Tovar hotel on the rim of the canyon is a must if you can get a table (see *Grand Canyon Sleeps & Eats*). You'll also want to **stay at one of the park hotels**, but make your reservations far in advance.

The next morning you can either take another hike (see Grand Canyon Best Activities) or **tour the West and East Rims**. All of the overlooks are wonderful, but some stand out for their special views. The **Abyss** is a highlight of the **West Rim** because here you can see the sheer Great Mojave Wall drop 3,000 feet straight down. This is only spot on the West Rim that you can see the Colorado River.

You'll leave the park via the 23-mile **East Rim Drive**. The over-looks here are spaced further apart than those of the West Rim and many of them are reached by spur roads. **Yaki Point** has some of the best canyon views in the park. **Moran** and **Lipan** points are unique because you're looking back into the canyon rather than down on it, which helps you appreciate its vastness. The **Desert View** overlook includes looks at not only the canyon, but also the Vermillion Cliffs, the San Francisco Peaks, and the Painted Desert.

LAKE POWELL/GLEN CANYON NATIONAL RECREATION AREA

After the busy days you've just had, Lake Powell is the perfect place to slow down the pace a bit. You'll spend two nights here to take in the beauty of this water wonderland.

En Route

After leaving the Grand Canyon, stop at the historic **Cameron Trading Post** on the way to Lake Powell. Have a meal here, do some shopping, or just browse the **incredible art gallery** with its extensive collection of rare and unique Native American pieces. *Info*: Just north of Cameron on US-89. Tel. 800-338-7385. www.camerontradingpost.com.

At Lake Powell

Lake Powell, created by the construction of the Glen Canyon Dam on the Colorado River, is a beautiful sapphire oasis amid stark striated cliffs. **Page**, the town on the edge of the lake, didn't even exist until construction of the dam began in 1956. The **Glen Canyon National Recreation Area** is a world-class water play-ground that encompasses much of the lake.

The only good way to see the area is by boat since only a small the portion of the incredible scen-ery is visible from land. Start your day with one of the **boat tours** offered at the Lake Powell Resort Marina. The most popu-lar trip, and justifiably so, is the all-day tour to **Rainbow Bridge National Monument,**

the largest known natural bridge in the world. Other tour options include half-day rides to both Navajo and Antelope Canyons or just a few hours cruising around the bay. *Info*: Tel. 800-528-6154. www.lakepowell.com. Prices vary from $50 to $115 for the different cruises.

You should also make a stop at the **Glen Canyon Dam Visitor Center**, located on the edge of the canyon wall. The structure and setting are most impressive. The outdoor observation deck offers looks at the river flowing hundreds of feet below. You can also take an elevator down to the dam's base for great views of the canyon walls. *Info*: Tel. 928-608-6404. Open daily 8am-5pm (7am-7pm in summer). Free admission.

MONUMENT VALLEY NAVAJO TRIBAL PARK
The iconic images of Monument Valley include sandstone monoliths as well as incredible freestanding rock formations.

En Route
It's worth detouring a few miles to visit the stunning **Navajo National Monument**. This park protects three amazing pueblo ruins that date from the 13th century. Sheltered beneath enormous cliffs, the ruins are an excellent condition. If you have the stamina, you should consider the ranger-led tours to either the Betatakin or Keet Seel ruins. Both involve difficult walks (five and sixteen miles), but are truly amazing. Even if you can't do the hike, there is a paved pathway from the visitor's center that affords great views of Betatakin. *Info*: Tel. 928-672-2700. www.nps.gov/nava/index.htm. Free entry.

At Monument Valley
Stop at the Visitor Center and then take the 17-mile self-guided **Valley Drive**, which winds through the many amazing rock formations found here. To access parts of the park not accessible without a guide, you can make arrangements at the visitor center parking lot for either **jeep or horseback tours**. If you have time, the Wildcat Trail is a wonderful three-mile hike that you can take on your own around the West Mitten Butte. *Info*: Tel. 435-727-5875. www.navajonationparks.org. Open daily 6am-8pm (May-September) or 8am-5pm (October-April.) $5 age 10 and over.

There's really only one choice for dinner and lodging near the park, **Goulding's Lodge**. Although Goulding's is actually located in Utah, it is very much a part of the Monument Valley environs. It's also worth a visit to tour their small museum and shop for Native American crafts at their gallery. *Info*: Tel. 435-727-3231. www.gouldings.com.

CANYON DE CHELLY
Located near Chinle, Canyon de Chelly, with deep red rocky walls and many historical ruins, is as beautiful as the Grand Canyon in its own way. Its smaller size makes it more intimate than the Grand Canyon. You'll spend two nights here to take in the sights both on the rim and in the canyon.

On the Rim
There are drives along both the north and south rims of the canyon. If you only have time for one drive, take the **South Rim**. Stop at the **White House Overlook**, where you can see the White House Ruin in the cliffs on the other side of the canyon. There is a **wonderful hiking trail** that leads down to the canyon floor from here. It is the only one you can take without a guide. It is steep but worth it if you are in shape.

Another don't miss spot on the South Rim is the **Spider Rock Overlook** at the end. Walk all the way out the overlook for an amazing view of Spider Rock, an 830 feet tall formation soaring up from the canyon floor.

In the Canyon
Spend your next day on the canyon floor taking a **guided tour**. You cannot enter the canyon without a guide, but the tours are easy to arrange and very informative. You can go with a group or have your own private tour. Sit back and enjoy the amazing scenery as your guide drives through deep sand on the canyon floor to some of the well-preserved cliff ruins. The green valley, dotted with Navajo farms, is one of the most peaceful spots you can imagine. It's best to arrange your tour in advance, but in slow seasons it is not necessary. *Info*: Arrange group guided trips at the Holiday Inn or Thunderbird Lodge for $48. Private 3-hour trips are $125 and must be arranged at the Holiday Inn. Call 800-679-2473 for reservations.

EASTERN ARIZONA'S WHITE MOUNTAINS
Today will be a day of contrast as your drive will take you from the stark, dry Painted Desert to one of the lushest spots in the state, Hannagan Meadow in the Apache-Sitgreaves National Forest.

En Route
From Canyon de Chelly, head south to I-40 and the **Petrified Forest National Park,** where crystallized mineral deposits have turned ancient trees into brightly colored petrified wood. The same minerals have also given the near by Painted Desert its amazing array of colors. Follow the 29-mile park road from the northern entrance just off I-40 to the exit on Highway 180.

The first section of road has a number of excellent overlooks that offer ever-changing views of the **Painted Desert** beyond. The **Newspaper Rock Overlook,** a little further along the route, offers views down at a huge sandstone rock covered with petroglyphs. There are a few easy walking paths through the petrified rocks that merit a stop, including the **Crystal Forest, Giant Logs**, and **Agate House** trails. *Info*: Off I-40 at exit 311. Tel. 928-524-6228. www.nps.gov/pefo. Open 8am-5pm daily. (7am-7pm in summer) $10 per vehicle.

From here take Highway 180 southeast to St. Johns and Highway 191. You will soon enter the **White Mountains**, which are generally contiguous with the Apache-Sitgreaves National Forest. These heavily forested, lush mountains are unique in Arizona. After passing through Springerville and Edgar, you begin a section of Highway 191 known as the **Coronado Trail**. The route purportedly follows that taken by Coronado in search of the Seven Cities of Gold. Regardless, it's a gorgeous, curvy drive along forests, meadows and lakes into the high mountains.

Hannagan Meadow
Remote Hannagan Meadow, located at 9100 feet elevation, is a wonderful spot to stay the night. You'll want to arrive while it's still light so that you can enjoy the beautiful scenery along the ride. There are literally thousands of acres of forests and trails near here as well as wonderful wildlife, including the recently

reintroduced gray wolf. The **Blue Range Primitive Area** is one of the best places in the state to get backcountry and away from it all (see *Eastern Arizona Best Activities*). Stay at the **Hannagan Meadow Lodge** or camp at the campground.

TUCSON

Your drive today will take you from the verdant and tree-covered White Mountains back down to the desert of Tuscon. You will spend a couple of days here exploring both the Sonoran Desert and the wonderful Hispanic culture of the city.

En Route

Continue south from Hannagan Meadow along the curvy and scenic Highway 191 until you reach I-10. Before you reach Tucson, exit at Benson to visit **Kartchner Caverns State Park**. This impressive system of pristine limestone caves was first discovered in 1974 and kept a secret for 14 years. The hour-long guided tour follows well-lit, paved paths through this fascinating underground world. Highlights include rooms the size of football fields as well as interesting cave formations. *Info*: AZ 90 south of Benson. www.azstateparks.com. Tel. 520-586-2283. Open 7:30am-6pm daily. $5 per car in addition to tour fees. Tours $23 adults, $13 children 7-13. Reservations recommended.

In Town

To gain a greater understanding of the desert around you, head to the **Arizona-Sonora Desert Museum**. This wonderful

Detour to Tombstone and Bisbee

If you'd rather stay above ground, consider a detour to Tombstone or Bisbee on your way into Tucson. Historic **Tombstone**, which appears much the same as it did in the 1880s, is a popular tourist destination. Among the many sights in town is the famous **OK Corral**, where the famous shoot out between the Earp Brothers and the Clanton Gang is reenacted on a daily basis. Further south is **Bisbee**, a picturesque community located in the southern mountains. You can tour the **Queen Mine** in an old mining car or just enjoy walking the streets of the funky little town.

attraction is a combination zoo and botanical garden focusing exclusively on species native to the region. Over 500 animals and birds roam and fly in their natural habitats. Kids and adults both will enjoy the many exhibits and habitat areas. *Info*: 2021 North Kinney Road. Tel. 580-883-2702. www.desertmuseum.org. Open 8:30am-5:30pm daily (7:30am in summer). Saturdays in summer open until 10pm. $12 adults. $4 children 6-12. (Discounted rates in summer.)

Next to the museum is the western portion of **Saguaro National Park**. Covered with thousands of towering Saguaro Cactus, the park is truly like a forest. If you want to explore the park on foot, the King Canyon Trail begins near the parking lot of the Arizona-Sonora Desert Museum. Don't miss the drive along **Kinney Road**, which winds through acres and acres of Arizona's green giants. *Info*: West Tucson: Tucson Mountain District. Tel. 520-733-5153. www.nps.gov/sagu. Open daily 7am-sunset. Visitor Center 9am-5pm. $10 per car.

Spend your afternoon exploring downtown Tucson's **Barrio Historico** and **El Presidio Historic District**. It is here that you truly appreciate the city's Spanish colonial past. Don't miss the **St. Augustine Cathedral**, modeled after the Cathedral of Queretaro in Mexico and the **Sosa-Carrillo-Fremont House**, an adobe-dwelling and museum complete with period furniture.

The **El Presidio Park Historic District** is the location of the original town site. Five historic homes that house collections of Western and Latin American art share the block with the **Tucson Museum of Art**. It's worth walking around down here even if you're not interesting in the exhibits to admire the wonderfully restored homes. *Info*: 140 North Main Avenue. Tel. 520-624-2333. www.tucsonarts.com. Open Tuesday-Saturday 10am-4pm. $8 adults. $3 children 13-18.

One of the highlights of Tucson is the wonderful downtown **Mexican restaurants**. Don't miss the chance to sip a cold margarita and enjoy the delicious food served here (see *Tucson Sleeps & Eats*).

The 320-acre campus of the **University of Arizona** has something for everyone. Sports fans can cheer for the many outstanding U of A athletic teams, shoppers will love the eclectic mix of stores lining nearby **4th Avenue**, while others will enjoy the school's great museums. The **Arizona State Museum** displays exhibits on the cultural development of the state. *Info*: www.statemuseum.arizona.edu. Tel. 520-621-6302 1013 E. University Boulevard. 10am-5pm Monday-Saturday, 12pm-5pm Sunday. Admission is free but a $3 donation is suggested. The **Center for Creative Photography**, with a collection of over 50,000 still pictures including the entire Ansel Adams catalog, is another favorite. *Info*: 1030 North Olive Road. Tel. 520-621-7968. www.creativephotography.org. Open 9am-5pm Monday-Friday, 12pm-5pm, Saturday-Sunday. Admission is free but a $5 donation is suggested.

PHOENIX

Your last day and half will be spent in the economic, governmental, and social center of the state. This is also a city of world-class resorts, so you'll want to spend a little R&R time in the Valley of the Sun.

In Phoenix

Visiting the **Heard Museum**, one of the world's most outstanding collections of southwestern art and culture, will be a wonderful way to end your trip after all the Native American culture you have experienced in the last two weeks. The lovely Spanish colonial building houses over **35,000 Native American objects** in several galleries. Don't miss the HOME: Native People's of the Southwest gallery. *Info*: 2103 N Central Ave. Tel. 602-252-8848. www.heard.org. Open daily 9:30am-5:00pm. Admission: $10 adults, $3 children 6-12.

Another wonderful Phoenix institution is the **Desert Botanical Garden**. Spread out over 145 acres, the Garden is a magnificent showcase for plant species from the world's most arid climates. The **Desert Discovery Trail** meanders 1/3 of a mile through the oldest and largest plantings in the garden. Check for special events which are frequently offered here. *Info*: 2101 N Galvin Parkway in Papago Park. Tel. 480-941-1225. www.dbg.org. Open daily October though April 8am-8pm; May-September 7am-8pm. Admission: $10 adults, $4 children 3-12.

Phoenix is known for its sunny days, so while you're here you should **spend some time outdoors**. Whether you want to golf, hike, bike or just lounge by the pool, there are many wonderful options (see *Phoenix Best Activities*).

Scattered around the Valley are a number of **world-class resorts**. You'll enjoy visiting one even if you're not staying there to tour the incredibly manicured grounds and wonderful facilities. Most offer spectacular views as well. You can enjoy a casual drink or meal in the outdoor living areas or go upscale at the wonderful restaurants. Try the Frank Lloyd Wright inspired **Arizona Biltmore and Villas** at the Camelback Corridor, the opulent **Phoenician** in Arcadia, or the elegant **Hyatt Gainey** in Scottsdale.

In Scottsdale
Fine arts fans should stop by the **Scottsdale Arts District**, where you'll find an amazing concentration of **outstanding galleries**. Marshall Way is the place for contemporary art, while cowboy and Native American works can be found a few blocks south on Main Street. There are also a number of boutiques and jewelry stores in the area.

Speaking of shopping, if you enjoy retail therapy then head to the new **Scottsdale Waterfront** area and the adjacent **Scottsdale Fashion Square Mall**. At the largest mall in the Southwest you'll find both national and local retailers as well as some outstanding local restaurants.

This part of **Old Town Scottsdale** is also **nightlife headquarters** for the Valley. There are many wonderful restaurants, bars and clubs for all tastes and demographics.

11. BEST SLEEPS & EATS

The entries below for Arizona's best hotels and restaurants follow the order of previous destination chapters. We've presented only the very best in each price category so you won't waste your time figuring out where to stay and eat! Expensive listings get three dollar signs, moderate get two, and inexpensive get one.

PHOENIX-SCOTTSDALE BEST SLEEPS

Arizona Biltmore Resort & Spa $$$
With a design influenced by **Frank Lloyd Wright**, the Biltmore has been a Valley favorite since it was built in the 1920s. Lots of stained glass and bright geometric designs. Spectacular grounds, with beautiful gardens ablaze with color, mountain vistas, and wicker lounge chairs for relaxing. There are **five pools**, one with a long water slide, two 18-hole golf courses, a full gym and steam room, and several **first-rate restaurants**. Rooms are large and comfortable and there are 78 suites with vaulted ceilings. Packages available. *Info*: www.arizonabiltmore.com. Tel. 800-950-0086.

Phoenix-Scottsdale

North Central Phoenix (Camelback Corridor) near the Phoenix Mountain Preserve: 2400 E Missouri Ave. 739 Rooms/Suites.

Fairmont Scottsdale Princess $$$
A luxurious larger-than-life **hacienda** situated on over 450 acres awaits you at the Princess. Designed in lovely **Mexican-colonial style**, the hotel features graceful arches and covered colonnades serving as walkways. Most spectacular is the large area from the main entrance back to the swimming pool – water cascades down pyramid-like structures while bridges lead over artificial streams. The wonderful rooms boast separate sleeping and living areas. Casitas and suites feature fireplaces. Dining at the Princess is a **gastronomic delight**. Both the **Marquesa** and **La Hacienda** should not be missed. Two golf courses, seven tennis courts, three **heated swimming pools**, a fitness trail, croquet and even fishing will keep you entertained, while the spa is a great place to relax. One of the best hotels in the state. *Info*: www.fairmont.com/scottsdale. Tel. 800-223-1818. North Scottsdale. 7575 East Princess Drive. 651 rooms.

Hyatt Regency Scottsdale at Gainey Ranch $$$
Low key and classy, the Hyatt is all about **understated elegance**. With a secluded palm-tree and cactus-lined driveway, the low-rise façade just hints at the beauty inside. The multi-level atrium lobby with retractable glass doors opens out to the magnificent grounds. The hotel's **outstanding collection of paintings**, statues and other works of art blend perfectly with the elegant shaded lounging areas. The rooms are large and comfortable and the restaurants are outstanding. Recreation opportunities include the full-service **Spa Avenia**, gym, tennis courts, 27 holes of championship golf, and trails for jogging or biking. A true gem. *Info*: www.scottsdale.hyatt.com. Tel. 800-233-1234. Central Scottsdale: 7500 East Doubletree Ranch Road. 493 Rooms/Suites.

Off-Season Specials

Trying to save a few bucks? Consider coming in the off season when you can get some **fantastic deals**. Rooms that go for $350 per night in the spring drop to $150 or less in the summer. Or, ask about the special golf or spa packages that many of the resorts offer.

architecture. A 2 1/2 acre **water playground** consists of ten interconnected swimming pools, a **white sand beach**, a three-story waterslide, glass and marble water cascades, and plenty of

The Phoenician $$$
European opulence meets southwest flavor at this luxury resort known for its **distinguished service**. Combines truly spectacular architecture with the natural beauty of its desert and mountain surroundings. A lush green oasis covering 250 acres. Admire the **dazzling lobby**, an exquisite mixture of marble, glass, and metal, highlighted by rich chandeliers, countless fountains, and numerous **impressive statues**. The shaded grounds are dominated by **seven cascading swimming pools** and a tropical lagoon. Even the smallest rooms are over 600 square feet and include **Italian marble bathrooms** and private balconies. Dining at the Phoenician is a big part of the experience. Don't miss the elegant Southern French cuisine at **Mary Elaine's**. Work off that dinner on the tennis courts, the 27-holes of golf, or the hiking and biking trails. The **Centre for Well-Being** includes a full gym as well as every spa treatment you can imagine. *Info*: www.thephoenician.com. Tel. 800-888-8234. Just a half-mile west of Old Town Scottsdale in Arcadia: 6000 East Camelback Road. 640 Rooms/Suites.

Royal Palms Resort & Spa $$$
Spanish-Mediterranean architecture in a truly remarkable setting. The small, **tranquil, and private** Royal Palms is as **genteel** as they come in the Valley. Tucked into the side of Camelback Mountain, the hotel still feels like the mansion it originally was. Built around quiet courtyards, the Royal Palms invites you to relax in style. The impeccably decorated guestrooms include custom furnishing, **fireplaces**, and private patios. **T. Cook's**, proclaimed the #1 restaurant in Phoenix by *Food & Wine Magazine*, lives up to its **lofty reputation**. A lovely, peaceful pool and full-service spa help visitors unwind. *Info*: www.royalpalmshotel.com. Tel. 800-672-6011. Right between Old Town Scottsdale and the Camelback Corridor in Arcadia: 5200 East Camelback Road. 117 Rooms/Casitas.

Wigwam Golf Resort & Spa $$$
Visit the Wigwam for a taste of Authentic Arizona. Originally

Phoenix-Scottsdale

built in 1918 as a getaway for visiting Goodyear executives, the Wigwam, on the west side of the valley, is a special property. The grounds are beautiful without being overdone, as are the public indoor areas. Both reflect the **appearance and atmosphere of a wealthy private home**. The guestrooms are some of the best in the state – **huge territorial-style casitas** with rich wood furniture decorated in the gentle tones of the surrounding desert. With **fireplaces** and native works of art they are truly extraordinary. Dining here is fantastic as well. The Wigwam specializes in R&R with three golf courses (two designed by **Robert Trent Jones,** tennis courts, horseback riding, and the new 16,000 square foot **Red Door Spa**. *Info*: www.wigwamresort.com. Tel. 800-327-0396. 16 miles west of downtown in Litchfield Park: 300 Wigwam Blvd. 331 casitas.

Golf Resorts

If **golf** is your main game and aim, you might consider two other fantastic hotels in the Scottsdale area. They are north of town and a bit isolated, but if you're looking for great golf, premium restaurants, and high-end spa facilities, you can't go wrong at two of the nation's premium golf resorts — The Four Seasons Resort (www.fourseasons.com/scottsdale/) or the Boulders Resort & Golden Door Spa (www.theboulders.com.)

Hotel Valley Ho $$

Enjoying a second heyday, the newly remodeled Valley Ho is once again the chic place to see and be seen. **Retro and cool**, the décor of the hotel stems from its original 60s look but updates it fantastically. Formerly a hangout for Hollywood's elite, the "Ho" is once again a Valley hotspot. In **easy walking distance to galleries, restaurant, and bars**, you can park your car and leave it. Don't miss **Café Zuzu**, a modern version of the 50s diner, or the OH poolside bar and cabanas. Flat screen TVs and balconies are standard in all the rooms. *Info*: www.hotelvalleyho.com. Tel. 866-882-4484. Old Town Scottsdale: 6850 E. Main Street. 200 Rooms.

Mondrian Hotel Scottsdale $$

An ultra-hip "**urban resort**," the Mondrian combines modern comfort with a **fantastic location** on the Scottsdale Civic Center Mall. Hang by the pool, workout at the gym, or get a massage in one of the open-air Treatment Cabanas. Rooms feature **plasma TVs** and deluxe sound systems. Enjoy Italian specialties at The Restaurant. Things get hopping at the **swank bar** once the sun goes down. *Info*: www.mondrianscottsdale.com. Tel. 800-697-1791. Old Town Scottsdale: 7353 East Indian School Road. 200 Rooms.

Maricopa Manor $$

An intimate B&B conveniently located near the famous "Camelback Corridor" of luxury shops and resorts. Great service and rooms for the price, with lots of old-world charm mixed with modern amenities. Small swimming pool and whirlpool. *Info*: www.maricopamanor.com. Tel. 800-292-6403. North Central Phoenix (Camelback Corridor): 15 West Pasadena Ave. 5 Rooms.

Pointe Hilton at Squaw Peak $$

Kids go nuts about this hotel. With six swimming pools, multiple waterfalls, and a **nine-acre water recreation** area called the Hole-in-the-Wall River Ranch, there is tons for them to be excited about. Especially big hits are the waterslides, miniature golf, and the "lazy river". The tough part will be getting them back to your **spacious room**. Rooms are arranged in small groups around a pool or courtyard, so it doesn't seem as if you're staying at such a large hotel. Other recreation includes golf, tennis, and a spa. *Info*: www.pointehilton.com. Tel. 800-947-9784. North Central Phoenix: 7677 N. 16th Street. 693 Rooms/Suites.

Hotel Waterfront Ivy $

A cozy boutique hotel in easy walking distance of Old Town Scottsdale. Situated **on the canal**, the hotel features **one and two-bedroom suites**. Multiple pools, a children's play area, and tennis courts make it a great place for families. There are even **fresh-baked cookies** every evening. *Info*: www.hotelwaterfrontivy.com. Tel. 877-770-7772. Old Town Scottsdale: 7445 East Chaparral Road. 125 Studios and Suites.

Motel 6 Scottsdale $

Yes, it's a Motel 6, but the **location is outstanding** and the **price**

couldn't be better for Scottsdale. An easy walk to shopping
galore at Scottsdale Fashion Square and Old Town. Small pool
with mountain views. *Info*: www.motel6.com. Tel. 800-466-8356.
Old Town Scottsdale: 6848 E Camelback Road. 122 Rooms.

Phoenix Inn Suites $
Just a block off Camelback road, the hotel is right in the **heart of
the action** but doesn't charge an arm and a leg for the privilege.
An all-suites hotel, it also features a **free breakfast buffet**, high
speed Internet, and **weeknight happy hour**. *Info*:
www.phoenixinnsuites.com/hotels/phoenix/index.htm. Tel.
800-956-5221. North Central Phoenix (Camelback Corridor): 2310
E Highland Ave. 120 Suites.

PHOENIX-SCOTTSDALE BEST EATS

Cowboy Ciao $$$
They call it "Modern American" food, but it's really an **inventive
union of Italian and Old West cuisine** that simply clicks. The
restaurant, decorated in Border Baroque style, is welcoming and
fun. Dinner will be as entertaining as it is delicious, especially if you
sample some of the generous pours from the extensive (over 2200
offerings) wine list. Yet the food remains the center of attention.
Don't miss the mushroom pan fry or the Elk Strip Loin. The Cuppa'
Red Hot Chocolate (cinnamon-spiked chocolate pot de crème with
ancho chile honey) justifies your entire trip to Phoenix. *Info*: Tel.
480-946-3111. Old Town Scottsdale: 7133 E. Stetson Dr. Open daily
lunch and dinner. Reservations recommended.

House of Tricks $$$
Located in side-by-side historic homes with a sprawling grape-
vine-canopied patio, House of Tricks is a **wonderful surprise
tucked into student-laden Tempe**. (Hey, professors have to eat
somewhere.) It's so pleasant you can't go wrong here for lunch,
dinner or even just happy hour. The menu takes advantage of
seasonally fresh ingredients and includes seafood, poultry, and
fine meats, as well as vegetarian selections. *Info*: Tel. 480-968-
1114. Tempe (near ASU): 114 East 7th Street. Closed Sunday.
Reservations recommended.

La Hacienda $$$

One of only two AAA Four-Diamond Mexican restaurants in North America, La Hacienda is a must for any trip to Phoenix. Located at the Scottsdale Princess in a turn-of-the-century Mexican ranch house, the setting alone is magnificent and worth seeing. The food however is the **most authentic and delicious central Mexican cuisine** I've had in Arizona. Try the house specialty, a spit-roasted suckling pig; or the broiled pacific lobster tail. Enjoy the live music, a strolling trio, as well as a fine list of aged tequilas. *Info*: Tel. 480-585-2721. North Scottsdale in the Scottsdale Princess Resort: 7575 E. Princess Drive. Reservations recommended.

Phoenix-Scottsdale

Lon's at the Hermosa $$$

You come to Lon's first for the incredible setting and ambiance and return again and again for the food. Housed in a historic hacienda (now the Hermosa Inn) in Paradise Valley, the wood and adobe dining room transports you to an earlier century. Even better however, is eating outside on the **expansive patio**, where you're surrounded by incomparable desert and mountain scenery. The menu, featuring inventive American cuisine and freshly harvested local produce, will make everybody happy. *Info*: Tel. 602-755-7878. Paradise Valley (between Old Town Scottsdale and the Camelback Corridor.) 5532 N. Palo Cristi Road. Open nightly for dinner and on weekdays for lunch. Reservations recommended.

T. Cook's $$$

Located in the incomparable mansion setting of the Royal Palms Hotel, T. Cook's offers **superb Mediterranean cuisine** influenced by northern Spain and central Italy. Voted the best restaurant in the Valley by *Food & Wine Magazine*, T. Cook's is a favorite for special occasions and celebrations. The Moroccan spiced scallops with Kabocha squash custard & vanilla butter sauce is a personal favorite. *Info*: Tel. 866-579-3636. Between the Camelback Corridor and Old Town Scottsdale in Arcadia: 5200 East Camelback Road. Open daily for breakfast lunch and dinner. Reservations recommended.

Vincent's on Camelback $$$
Exquisite cuisine and service in a memorably romantic atmosphere. There's a hint of **both French and southwest** in everything on the menu – a most appealing and flavorful combination despite how it might sound.

Many entrees are mesquite grilled. Especially delicious are the grilled rack of lamb with thyme, rosemary, garlic and spicy pepper jelly and the corn ravioli with white truffle oil. *Info*: Tel. 602-224-0225. Camelback Corridor: 3930 East Camelback Road. Closed Sundays. Reservations recommended.

Vincent's Market Bistro

If a fancy French meal is too heavy on your wallet, try the attached Vincent's Market Bistro. You can sample much of the same cuisine at a fraction of the cost.

Barrio Café $$
For delicious **southern Mexico cuisine in a very lively atmosphere**, don't miss the justifiably popular Barrio Café. The guacamole prepared tableside is outstanding, as is the *cochinita pibil*, Yucatan-style pork roasted with achiote and oranges. You'll probably have to wait a while for a table, but half the fun is ordering drinks and appetizers in the tiny bar. *Info*: Tel. 602-636-0240. Central Phoenix: 2814 N. 16th Street (1 1/2 blocks south of Thomas.) Open for dinner Tuesday-Sunday and lunch Tuesday-Friday. Sunday Brunch. Closed Mondays. No reservations.

Café Zuzu $$
Zuzu serves what it calls comfort food, but chances are pretty good it's not the way your mama made it. This "diner" is actually a swank and fun hangout inside the newly remodeled Hotel Valley Ho. A 50's soda fountain updated for the 21st century, Zuzu has **reinvigorated classics** like Mac-n-cheese, meatloaf, and tuna noodle casserole. Desserts from the soda fountain are delicious as well. *Info*: Tel. 866-882-4484. Old Town Scottsdale: 6850 E. Main Street. Open daily. Reservations accepted.

Chelsea's Kitchen $$
Once an old roadhouse, this landmark building on the canal in

Arcadia is now one of Phoenix's most enjoyable eateries. With a **fantastic patio** and nice open floor plan, the restaurant is comfortable yet chic at the same time. While it's a hot spot for couples, it's also great for families because it's **plenty lively**. Try the lobster tacos or the melt-in-your-mouth braised short ribs. *Info*: Tel. 602-957-2555. Arcadia (between Old Town Scottsdale and the Camelback Corridor): 5040 N. 40th Street – 40ᵗʰ just north of Camelback. Open daily for dinner only. No reservations.

Phoenix-
Scottsdale

La Grande Orange Pizzeria and Grocery $$
It's a pizzeria, a grocery store, a cafe, a coffeehouse, and a wine store – if you can't make everybody in your group happy here then you can't make them happy anywhere. A popular neighborhood haunt, La Grande Orange features casual seating outdoors and a contemporary urban vibe inside. With great pizza, pastries, sandwiches, salads and breakfasts **you can't go wrong any time of day**. (The pizzeria is only open at dinner however.) *Info*: Tel. 602-840-7777. Arcadia (between Old Town Scottsdale and the Camelback Corridor): 40th Street & Campbell at 3939 East Campbell. Open daily. No reservations.

Pizzeria Bianco $$
Calling Pizzeria Bianco a "pizza joint" is a bit like calling a Stradivarius "a nice fiddle." Owner Chris Bianco was named by the James Beard Foundation as the **best chef in the southwest – for his pizza!** Made with homemade crust, fresh mozzarella, and herbs straight from the garden, these are pizzas you will dream about when you're back home. There is always a wait, but luckily there are picnic tables outside where you can bring wine from Bar Bianco next door and enjoy the historic atmosphere of Heritage Square. *Info*: Tel. 602-258-8300. Downtown in Heritage Square: 623 E Adams. Open for dinner only. Closed Sunday and Monday. Reservations for groups of 6-10 only.

Best Gourmet Pizza

Besides La Grande Orange and Pizzeria Bianco, two other great gourmet pizza restaurants are Cibo (603 North Fifth Ave at Fillmore St, Tel. 602-441-2697) and Grazie (6952 E Main St, Scottsdale, Tel. 480-663-9797).

The Restaurant at Mondrian $$
Located right on the Scottsdale Civic Center Mall inside of the
Mondrian Hotel, The Restaurant **works well for breakfast,
brunch, lunch or dinner.** The daytime menu is on the lighter side,
featuring sandwiches and salads, while the nighttime menu is
full of Italian specialties. Both change often and feature seasonal
ingredients. *Info*: Tel. 480-308-1111. Old Town Scottsdale: 7353
East Indian School Road. Open daily. Reservations accepted.

Art Museum Café by Arcadia Farms $
Featuring organically grown vegetables, the Art Café inside the
wonderful Phoenix Art Museum, is a great place to relax and eat
lunch. Gourmet sandwiches and salads, as well as wonderful
pastries, make it **worth a stop even if you're not going to tour the
museum.** *Info*: Tel. 257-2191. Downtown at Central and McDowell:
1625 N Central Ave. Open Tuesday-Sunday. No reservations.

AZ88 $
With a **fantastic location** right on the Scottsdale Civic Center
Mall, the patio of AZ88 overlooks fountains, gardens, and quite
often, shows at the amphitheater. With a simple but tasty menu
of salad, sandwiches, and burgers, the restaurant draws a crowd
that changes as the night progresses. The families give way to
couples and groups of singles, which give way to partiers with
the munchies the later it gets. *Info*: Tel. 480-994-5576. Old Town
Scottsdale: 7353 Scottsdale Mall. Open weekdays for lunch and
dinner. Open for dinner only on weekends. No reservations.

Café at the Biltmore & Squaw Peak Lounge $
With open air seating under the portico, the Café and Lounge at
the Biltmore are a **great way to experience a luxury resort
without harming your wallet.** It's all about the ambiance. You
look out over the incredible manicured gardens to see the peaks
of the Phoenix Mountain Preserve beyond. You can wait for a
server, but it's easier to go inside the café and order a sandwich
or salad yourself. They'll bring it out to you when it's ready and
in the meantime you will have been mesmerized by the view.
Info: Tel. 602-381-7632. North Central Phoenix (Camelback Cor-
ridor) near the Phoenix Mountain Preserve: 2400 E Missouri Ave.
Open daily for breakfast and lunch. No reservations.

My Florist Café $

Open literally all day long, My Florist is a **chic neighborhood restaurant** that draws people from all over the Valley. The menu features gourmet sandwiches and salads as well as wonderful pastries and breakfast items. On Wednesday though Sunday evenings an incredible pianist entertains patrons on the Steinway. Definitely worth a visit if you're in the neighborhood. *Info*: Tel. 602-254-0333. Downtown Phoenix (5th Ave and McDowell): 534 West McDowell. Open daily 7am-midnight. Reservations for parties of 8 or more.

Phoenix-
Scottsdale

Tucson

Postino Winecafe $

Postino is like a commercial for how happy hour is supposed to be – **pretty people drinking excellent wines and noshing on tasty fare.** Housed in what used to be the Arcadia post office, the building has a glass paneled garage door that is rolled up in nice weather to create a wonderful indoor/outdoor effect. Postino serves excellent light dishes of bruschetta, salads, and panini and of course, the wine is divine. Even though it is hip, it is not really a place to see and be seen. It's more a place to come and enjoy. *Info*: Tel. 602-852-3939. Arcadia (between Old Town Scottsdale and the Camelback Corridor): 40th Street & Campbell at 3939 East Campbell. Closed Sunday. No reservations.

TUCSON BEST SLEEPS

Arizona Inn $$$

One of the state's oldest luxury resorts, the Arizona Inn has been pampering guests since 1930. The Inn provides a **secluded and private desert oasis** on 14-acres in the middle of the city. **Adobe-style buildings** and cottages house a small number of guests, so you get personalized service. Includes a beautifully landscaped courtyard with a rich, carpet-like lawn dotted with flowers. The warmly decorated rooms have balconies or patios and **many have fireplaces**. Facilities include two tennis courts, croquet, and exercise equipment along with the heated pool. **Excellent restaurants and library.** *Info*: www.arizonainn.com. Tel. 800-933-1093. University of Arizona Area: 2200 E. Elm St. 83 rooms.

Canyon Ranch $$$

More a health-retreat than hotel, the Canyon Ranch is world-famous for its spa and fitness programs. Built in harmony with the desert terrain, the accommodations range from deluxe rooms to master suits. All are decorated in a classy southwestern style. Some visitors are here to rest, relax and rejuvenate with the many spa services, while others enjoy the **extensive recreation opportunities** including hiking, aquatics, tennis, and every type of yoga or fitness class you can imagine. You can even get a physical while you're here. Must be 14. Alcohol not permitted on site. Four-night minimum stay. All meals included. *Info*: www.canyonranch.com/resorts. Tel. 800-742-9000. Northeast Tucson: 8600 E. Redrock Cliff Rd. 240 rooms.

The Lodge at Ventana Canyon $$$

The **epitome of luxurious living,** the spacious suites are done in an elegant southwest motif that would be hard to improve upon. Many of the units have two bedrooms, making it a great place for families. Almost every unit overlooks the beautiful Catalina Mountains as the Lodge is **picturesquely situated in the foothills.** The many recreational facilities include 36 holes of golf, 12 tennis courts, and a spa. *Info*: www.thelodgeatventanacanyon.com. Tel. 800.828.5701. Northeast Tucson: 6200 North Clubhouse Lane. 49 rooms.

Tanque Verde Ranch $$$

One of the fine Arizona guest ranches, Tanque Verde is a historic **working cattle ranch** with all of the ranch activities you would expect. Situated on 640 acres in the Rincon Mountains near Saguaro National Park East, the ranch boasts a stable of over 150 horses. There are **many riding and lesson opportunities available each day,** including trail rides, walking rides for beginners, and loping rides. Tennis and spa services are available. There is also a **pool and evening entertainment**, plus an excellent children's program starting at age 4. The 74 guest units range from standard rooms to suites. Most have a fireplace and patio. All meals are included in the rates and they are very good. *Info*: www.tanqueverderanch.com. Tel. 800-234-3833. Northeast Tucson: 14301 E Speedway Blvd. 74 rooms.

Westin La Paloma $$$
This beautiful Spanish Mission style resort is built into the hillside **at the foot of the Catalina Mountains**. The grounds are gorgeous and are highlighted by the **huge pool area** that has a magnificent waterfall, a waterslide, and a **swim-up bar and grill**. Other recreational facilities include a fitness center, tennis courts, and 27 holes of golf. The **guestrooms and suites are some of the best in the city**, as they are huge and recently updated with a warm, golden color-scheme. The restaurants are also top-notch, as is the **not-to-be-missed J-Bar**. *Info*: www.westinlapaloma.com. Tel. 800-876-3683. North Tucson: 3800 East Sunrise Drive. 487 rooms.

Lowe's Ventana Canyon $$$
Spread out over almost **90 beautifully landscaped acres at the foot of the Catalinas**, the property provides magnificent views of both mountain and city. While natural flora abound, the show-case of the grounds is an **80-foot waterfall** that leads into a "river" that travels serenely throughout the grounds of the resort. **Guestrooms are large and attractive** without being over-the-top, and some suites have full kitchens. The **dining facilities are excellent** as well. All the recreation opportunities you could want are here – pools, health club, tennis courts, and golf as well as a **jogging trail and nature path**. Free shuttle to Sabino Canyon. *Info*: http://www.loewshotels.com/hotels/tucson/. Tel. 800-234-5117. Northeast Tucson: 7000 North Resort Dr. 398 rooms.

Hacienda del Sol Guest Ranch $$-$$$
The Hacienda del Sol is a **cross between a luxury resort and a more casual guest ranch** with great mountain views. This hotel exudes a warm Old World charm throughout the historic haci-enda-style buildings. The 31 rooms are located on a spacious **34-acres of meticulously cared for grounds**. An oasis of tranquility and beauty, you could spend many hours just letting time float by as you casually wander around. **Oversized rooms** are the rule with the décor in keeping with the hacienda atmosphere. Swim-ming pool, spa, tennis and horseback riding. *Info*: www.haciendadelsol.com. Tel. 800-728-6514. 5601 N. Hacienda del Sol Road. 31 rooms.

White Stallion Ranch $$-$$$

For a true western encounter, the **White Stallion Ranch cannot be beat**. The 3,000 acre ranch opened its doors to guests 1965 and has really **figured out how to deliver a wonderful guest ranch experience**. Located in the Tucson Mountains adjacent to Saguaro National Park West, the White Stallion is run by some of the friendliest most down-to-earth people in the state. The **riding programs are outstanding,** including up to four rides daily, as are the evening entertainment sessions. The rooms, decorated in western motif, are very comfortable. The swimming pool is a favorite spot for congregating after rides. Happy hour in the bar, **complete with saddles for barstools,** is a fun nightly ritual, as is the evening entertainment. The meals are very good. Rates **include lodging, all meals, horseback rides, and use of recreational facilities. Massages are extra. Open September-May.** *Info*: www.wsranch.com. Tel. **888-977-2624. Northwest Tucson: 9251 W. Twin Peaks Rd.** 32 rooms.

El Conquistador Hilton $$-$$$

The El Conquistador, nestled in the foothills of the Santa Catalinas, is a **wonderful resort for vacationing families who want it all.** With extensive pool and waterslide facilities, three golf courses, tennis courts, and a spa, everyone will be more than happy. The guestrooms and suites are large and comfortable and there is a **nice array of dining options**, including Nuevo Latino, casual poolside, and a fun western steakhouse and music hall. *Info*: www.hiltonconquistador.com. Tel. 800-325-7832. Northwest Tucson: 10000 North Oracle Road. 428 rooms.

El Presidio Bed & Breakfast Inn $$

The inn's **1880's adobe-style mansion fits** in perfectly with the rest of El Presidio Historic District. The inn is spacious and the grounds are simply gorgeous with a **lush garden and courtyard** featuring cobblestone walkways and a beautiful fountain. The **large suites — two with kitchens —** are attractively furnished. The breakfast is gourmet and in the evening your hosts invite you to beverages and fresh fruit. Some restrictions on small children. *Info*: www.bbonline.com/az/elpresidio/index.html. Tel. 800-349-6151. **El Presidio Historic District:** 297 N. Main Avenue. Full breakfast included. 4 suites.

Peppertrees Bed & Breakfast Inn $$
This pretty Victorian residence, built in 1905, is located **on a quiet street close to everything**. All of the rooms are **filled with antiques** dating back to turn-of-the-century Tucson. There are five large bedroom units and two larger southwestern-style guest houses. Guests receive a **hearty gourmet breakfast** personally prepared by the owner as well as warm and friendly service. *Info*: www.peppertreesinn.com. Tel. 800-348-5673. University of Arizona Area: 724 East University Blvd. Full breakfast included. 7 rooms.

Tucson

Adobe Rose Inn $$
Located in an adobe house built in 1933, the Adobe Rose feels **very authentically Tucson**. The spacious guest facilities are surrounded by a **small but lushly planted central patio**. Both the rooms and larger cottages are charmingly furnished. Two of the rooms feature fireplaces and the cottages have efficiency kitchens. Small pool. No children under 10. *Info*: www.aroseinn.com. Tel. 800-328-4122. University of Arizona Area: 940 Olsen Avenue. 6 rooms.

Hotel Congress $
This historic hotel in the heart of downtown is the **epicenter of hip Tucson**. While the rooms are pure vintage southwestern charm, including antique iron beds and an operational switchboard, the **restaurant and nightclub are cutting edge rock and roll**. Cable TV but no in-room telephones. *Info*: www.hotelcongress.com. Tel. 800-722-8848. Downtown: 311 E. Congress St. 40 rooms.

La Posada Lodge and Casitas $-$$
A **wonderful boutique hotel**, La Posada offers quite a lot for the price. The rooms are nicely decorated in Santa Fe style, while the 12 casitas offer space and comfort. With a **pool, exercise room, and nice Mexican restaurant on site**, you get some of the amenities of a resort. *Info*: www.laposadalodge.com. Tel. 800-810-2808. Northwest Tucson: 5900 North Oracle Road. 72 rooms.

Wayward Winds Lodge $
A **friendly, family-run establishment**, the Wayward Winds is a **simple but attractive motel**. All of the guestrooms overlook an

attractively landscaped courtyard, and there are even apartment units with refrigerators for a slightly higher price. **Heated swimming pool, shuffleboard, and barbeque area**. *Info*: Tel. 800-791-9503. Northwest Tucson: 707 West Miracle Mile. 40 rooms.

TUCSON BEST EATS

Anthony's in the Catalinas $$$
Anthony's hallmark is **expertly prepared continental cuisine** served with great style and efficiency. The restaurant is beautiful, as are the **mountain and city views**. The wine selection, from their own cellars, is outstanding, making them a Wine Spectator Grand Award winner. *Info*: Tel. 520-299-1771. Eastside: 6440 N. Campbell Ave. Open for dinner nightly. Reservations recommended.

Arizona Inn Main Dining Room $$$
Featuring **outstanding service and fine continental cuisine**, the Arizona Inn is a wonderful option if you don't want to make the trek out to some of the high-end restaurants in the foothills. The decor is **Old World elegance**, with cathedral ceilings, a fireplace, and a courtyard. The beef tenderloin is deliciously prepared, as is the salmon. Enjoy an after dinner drink in the dignified Audubon Bar, featuring **live piano music** nightly. *Info*: Tel. 520-325-1541. University of Arizona Area: 2200 E. Elm St. Open nightly for dinner. Reservations recommended.

Janos $$$
An **extraordinary dining experience** awaits you in this historic adobe pueblo constructed in the 1850s and now designated a national landmark. While it's the food that brings people here, the furnishings and service are equally spectacular. The inspired cuisine is **southwestern with a French influence**. The menu is very much determined by what is fresh and in season. Much of the seafood **is flown in fresh from the Sea of Cortez**. The selections of wines have been carefully chosen to perfectly complement the menu. *Info*: Tel. 520-615-6100. Eastside at the Westin La Paloma: 3770 East Sunrise Drive. Open for dinner only. Closed Sunday. Reservations recommended.

The Ventana Room $$$

Among the most sophisticated dining spots in the state, the Ventana Room offers **elegant surroundings and exquisite views** of the city. After dark, especially, it is a superb setting for a delicious meal. The beautifully prepared and presented continental cuisine is outstanding. The exceeding knowledgeable staff is professional and quite formal. *Info*: Tel.520-299-2020. Eastside at the Loew's Ventana Canyon: 7000 N. Resort Drive. Open for dinner nightly. Reservations recommended.

Tucson

Café Poca Cosa $$

Definitely **one of the best Mexican food restaurants in the city**, Cafe Poca Cosa serves extremely **imaginative, pleasingly prepared** Mexican specialties. The menu changes twice daily, so you'll probably be tempted to eat here more than once. The tamales, a constant on the menu, are outstanding, as are the mole sauces. Whatever you order, you're such to enjoy this take on **Mexican high cuisine**. The original location, on South Scott, is only open on weekdays for breakfast and lunch. The newer location, right around the corner on Broadway, is attached to the Clarion Hotel. *Info*: Tel. 520-622-6400. Downtown: 88 E Broadway and 20 S. Scott. Lunch and dinner Monday-Saturday. Closed Sunday. Dinner reservations recommended.

Café Terra Cotta $$

Café Terra Cotta serves **fantastic modern southwestern cuisine**. The dishes, which change weekly, are prepared using **fresh and mostly local ingredients**. The dining room is comfortable and casual, with turquoise and copper accents and large view windows. Even better much of the year is the **outdoor patio**. The **food here is equally as good as served that by the fanciest restaurants in town**. If you're not in the mood for a full meal, try their wood-fired pizza – I know it's not southwestern, but it's delicious. *Info*: Tel. 520-577-8100. Eastside: 3500 Sunrise Dr. Open daily starting at 4pm. Sunday brunch 10am-3pm. Dinner reservations recommended.

Caruso's $$

Caruso's, **in the heart of 4th Ave**, is somewhat of a local legend for expertly preparing Italian fare since 1938. The menu selections aren't fancy – pizza, ravioli, lasagna, manicotti – but they are all just about as good as you can make them and are served in generous amounts. Try getting a table on the beautiful **patio surrounded by a refreshing row of shade trees**. A delightful experience. *Info*: Tel. 520-624-5765. University of Arizona Area: 434 N. 4th Ave. Dinner served nightly except Monday.

El Charro Cafe $$
The original El Charro on Court Avenue has been serving guests since 1922 and claims to be the **oldest Mexican restaurant in the country**. It's a tough call whether this or Café Poca Cosa is the best Mexican restaurant in town. You certainly **can't go wrong** at either one. El Charro features **authentic Sonoran-style food**, which is very hard to find in many part of the US. The *carne seca*, which they dry on the roof in the traditional manner, is outstanding. The atmosphere here is great here as well — **order your margarita in a boot** and you get to take the glass home for free! *Info*: Downtown: 311 N Court Ave: Tel. 520-622-1922; North: 100 W. Orange Grove. Tel. 520-615-1922. Speedway: 4699 E. Speedway. Tel. 520-325-1922. Open daily for lunch at dinner.

J-Bar $$
Located in the same building as its sister restaurant Janos, the J-Bar serves **fantastic food and drinks at a more accessible price**. It has a very pretty patio where you can watch the Tucson city lights twinkling below while consuming **tasty Latin-Caribbean cuisine**. Most of the offerings come straight off the grill. The **drinks here are fantastic and come from all over Latin America** – mojitos, sangria, and even Mexican micheladas. Don't miss the summer music series on Wednesday and Thursday nights. *Info*: Tel. 520-615-6100. Eastside at the Westin La Paloma: 3770 East Sunrise Drive. Opens 5pm nightly. Closed Sunday.

Montana Avenue $$
The latest edition to the very popular family of Fox Restaurants, Montana Avenue features **comfort food updated with a southwestern twist**. The interior is super cool, with custom-made wooden tables and cowhide chairs. The patios, with fireplaces, are also very pleasant places to eat. Montana Avenue's **sister restaurants**, **Wildflower**, featuring New American Cuisine and

Bistro Zin, a French-inspired bistro and wine bar, are also high-lights of the Tucson culinary scene. *Info:* Tel. 520.298.2020. Eastside: 6390 E. Grant Road. Open for lunch and dinner daily. Dinner reservations recommended.

Olive Tree $$
The Olive Tree serves up **some of the best Greek food in Tucson.** The menu features a diverse selection of continental dishes and seafood in addition to **traditional Greek favorites** like mousaka and spanakopita. The indoor dining room features an attractive Mediterranean-style décor and the **courtyard patio is simply delightful.** Olive Tree also boasts an impressive list of European and domestic wines. *Info:* Tel. 520-298-1845. Eastside: 7000 E Tanque Verde Road. Open nightly for dinner.

The B-line $
A **wonderful bistro on 4th Ave,** the B-line really can't be beat for a casual breakfast, lunch, or dinner. The **homemade pies, cakes, and cookies** will have you stopping by again and again whenever you're in the area, as will the catfish burro. *Info:* Tel. 882-7575. University of Arizona Area: 621 N. Fourth Ave. Open 7am-10pm. Closed Mondays.

Beyond Bread $
Beyond Bread does indeed go far beyond bread. **Amazing salads, sandwiches and pastries** make either location a great stop for any meal. The **sandwiches, made on their homemade bread, are big enough for two.** *Info:* Both locations on Eastside: 6260 E. Speedway Blvd. Tel. 520-747-7477; 3026 N. Campbell Ave. Tel. 520-322-9965. Mon-Fri 6:30am-8:00pm, Sat 7:00am-8:00pm, Sun 7:00am-6:00pm.

Cup Café $
Located in the historic Hotel Congress, the Cup Café is **a hit for breakfast, lunch or dinner.** While the menu seems to be all over the place, with Asian, Latin, and American influences, the food is top-notch. **Hip Tucson hangs out here,** which must explain with specialty cocktails are so outstanding. *Info:* Tel. 800-798-1618. Downtown: 311 E. Congress St. Open 7am-10pm daily. (11 pm weekends.)

Magpies Gourmet Pizza $
When one restaurant wins a Best of Tucson award for 17 years you know they are doing something right. Magpies Pizza is that restaurant. The pizza is the draw of course, but they also serve excellent calzones and salads. Six locations around town, including 4th Ave and 5th Street right by the University. *Info*: Tel. 520-628-1661. University of Arizona: 605 N. 4th Ave.

NORTH-CENTRAL ARIZONA BEST SLEEPS & EATS

FLAGSTAFF
Inn at 410 $$
Winner of numerous awards, this B&B is located in a large two-story home a **few short blocks from Flag's historic downtown district**. The structure, built in 1907, is on a **quiet street** with nicely shaded grounds that include a small garden. Each room is decorated in a unique manner and features the southwestern décor of an earlier era. **Breakfast is abundant, wholesome and delicious.** *Info*: www.inn410.com. Tel. 800-774-2008. Downtown: 410 N. Leroux Street. 9 rooms.

Little America Hotel $$
This classic lodge hotel is located on a **magnificent 500-acre ponderosa forest** with views of the San Francisco Mountains to the north. Guest accommodations are spread out in several buildings that go well with the natural surroundings. **The rooms are unusually large**. A large swimming pool and play area, along with the woods, make it a **fun place for kids**. There are hiking trails and a gym, along with three restaurants. *Info*: www.littleamerica.com/flagstaff. Tel. 800-865-1401. East of downtown: 2515 East Butler Ave. 247 rooms.

Hotel Monte Vista $
If you want to **experience historic Flagstaff**, and can sleep through some train noise, the Monte Vista, in the heart of downtown is for you. Over a hundred movies were filmed in and around Northern Arizona during the 40s and 50s and **many Hollywood stars spent time here**. Some of the rooms are named

after these famous visitors. *Info*: www.hotelmontevista.com. Tel. 800-545-3068. Downtown: 100 N. San Francisco St. 48 rooms.

FLAGSTAFF BEST EATS
The Cottage Place $$$
A long-time favorite and excellent choice for continental cuisine, wine and atmosphere. Great **tasting menu** on weekends. A little more formal than Josephine's. Wine Spectator award of excellence winner. *Info*: Tel. 928-774-8431. Two blocks south of downtown off Beaver: 126 West Cottage Avenue. Open for dinner Tuesday-Sunday. Reservations recommended.

Josephine's $$$
Great modern American food and wine served in a historic Craftsman bungalow. Far better food than you would expect out of a crunchy college town. **Delightful outdoor seating** in summer and two indoor fireplaces for winter. Wine Spectator award of excellence winner. *Info*: Tel. 928-779-3400. Downtown: 503 N. Humphrey's Street. Open daily in summer; closed Sunday rest of year. Reservations recommended.

La Bellavia $
The entire menu is a winner, but breakfast is especially popular. Don't miss the **Swedish oat pancakes**. If you like sausage, the chorizo scramble will put you over the top. *Info*: Tel. 928-774-8301. Two blocks south of downtown on Beaver. 18 S Beaver St. Open for breakfast and lunch daily.

Cheap Eats in Flagstaff

Here are some of the best in the budget category and they are all pretty close to campus:
- **El Charro** – Darn good Sonoran-Mexican. (Tel. 928-779-0552. 409 S San Francisco St.)
- **Alpine Pizza** - Extremely casual with pool table and TVs. (Tel. 928-779-4109. 7 N Leroux St.)
- **Bunhuggers** – Great burgers and shakes. (Tel. 928-779-3743. 901 S Milton Rd # A1.)

Macy's European Coffee House $
A coffee house, bakery and vegetarian restaurant, Macy's pretty

much sums up the Flagstaff vibe. Definitely worth a visit. *Info*: Tel. 928-774-2243. Two blocks south of downtown on Beaver. 14 S Beaver St, Flagstaff. Open Daily 6am-8pm (10pm Thurs-Sat.)

Salsa Brava $
My family's choice for the **best Mexican food** in town. The salsas are made from scratch daily, as are the rest of the menu items. Don't miss the Maui tacos or the carnitas. *Info*: Tel. 928-779-5293. On the east side of town on Route 66. 2220 E Route 66. Open for lunch and dinner daily.

Beef Jerky & Heineken

For an example of why we love Flagstaff, check out the Pay-n-Take (Tel. 928-226-8595, 12 W Aspen Ave.) Where else can you find a convenience store with a full bar? Draft and bottled beer, wine by the bottle or glass, and your standard convenience store inventory. Good place to watch sporting events too...especially the Tour de France.

Beaver Street Brewery $
Great micro-brews, fun atmosphere, and hearty burgers and pizza. **Delicious and appropriate for all ages**. Nice outdoor seating. *Info*: Tel. 928-779-0079. Two blocks south of downtown on Beaver: 11 S. Beaver St., No. 1.

JEROME BEST SLEEPS & EATS
Jerome Grand Hotel $$
Located in a historic five-story Spanish mission structure, the Jerome Grand Hotel perches at the top of town. The beautifully restored rooms offer **fantastic views**. If you enjoy hotels with **character**, this is the place for you. Don't miss the **excellent Asylum restaurant** as well. *Info*: www.jeromegrandhotel.net. Tel. 888-817-6788. 200 Hill St.

The Asylum at the Jerome Grand Hotel $$$
Have a **drink on the patio** and enjoy the views before making your way inside to a wonderful dining experience. Start with the squash soup and you won't be disappointed. **Wine Spectator Award of Excellence** winner. *Info*: Tel. 928-639-3197. Above town: 200 Hill St. Open daily for lunch and dinner.

Haunted Hamburger

If **good food in a casual environment** is what you're after, you'll find it here. Try the gourmet burgers on the **outdoor deck** and follow them up with the chocolate cake. *Info*: Tel. 928-634-0554. Downtown: 410 N Clark Street.

Jerome
—
Prescott

PRESCOTT BEST SLEEPS

Hassayampa Inn $$

This **historic property** dates from 1927 and fits in perfectly with the surroundings of Court House Square and its old shops and buildings. **Exudes charm** and comfort, although most of the rooms are on the smallish size. Try breakfast at the hotel's Peacock room. (The inn is **purported to be haunted** be a ghost named Faith.) *Info*: www.hassayampainn.com. Tel. 800-322-1927. Downtown: 122 E Gurley St. 68 rooms.

Mt. Vernon Inn $$

This historic inn was built in the early 1900s. A **charming place on a tree-shaded block** that contains many Victorian style homes, the Mt. Vernon is noted for its **outstanding architectural features**. The main house has a large and comfortable parlor where guests can meet and mingle or just relax. All of the rooms and cottages are distinctively furnished. *Info*: Tel. 928-778-0886. Near downtown: 204 North Mount Vernon Ave. 4 guestrooms and 3 cottages.

Hotel St. Michael $

Located right in the heart of Whiskey Row, the St. Michael is not for those who want tranquility. If you want to be a **part of the action** however, this is the place for you. The rooms are old-fashioned (i.e. on the small side), but you can inquire about a suite if you need more space. **Breakfast at the wonderful Caffe St. Michael included.** *Info*: www.stmichaelhotel.com. Tel. 800-678-3757. Downtown: 205 W Gurley St. 72 rooms.

PRESCOTT BEST EATS

Iron Springs Café $$

Housed in the historic depot building, the Iron Springs Café is definitely a local favorite. It's not right in the center of town, so few tourists wander in, but it's very popular anyway. With

Southwest and Cajun influences, dishes like the garlic shrimp tamales are fantastic. *Info*: Tel. 928-443-8848. West of downtown: 1501 W Iron Springs Rd.

Murphy's Restaurant $$
Murphy's is located in a refurbished commercial building dating from the 1890s in the **heart of Prescott's historic downtown**. Good mesquite broiled meat dishes as well as **wonderful home baked bread**. They are also known for their huge selection of domestic and imported beers. *Info*: Tel. 928-445-4044. Downtown: 201 North Cortez St. Lunch and dinner served daily. Sunday brunch.

Bin 239 $$
This little **wine-cafe** is a great Prescott asset. Enjoy wonderful **wood-fired pizza**, fresh salads, and an extensive wine list. **Desserts are primo** as well. *Info*: Tel. 928-445-3855. Downtown: 239 N Marina St.

Dinner Bell $
Although they have "dinner" in the name, this is **the spot for breakfast**. If you want hearty and lots of options, come here. *Info*: Tel. 928-445-9888. Downtown: 321 W Gurley St. Open for breakfast and lunch until 2pm daily.

SEDONA BEST SLEEPS
Enchantment Resort $$$
This beautiful resort is located in a private area of a secluded canyon. The hotel is **enveloped by and blends in with the natural red rock formations** that have made Sedona famous. Spread out in many different small buildings, the guestrooms are all individual suites or more elaborate casitas. The views are amazing. Offers a **host of recreational activities**, including five swimming pools, a pitch & putt course, croquet and tennis. The outstanding Yavapai Restaurant is worth a trip even if you're not staying here. The Mii Amo **spa is also a huge draw**. *Info*: www.enchantmentresort.com. Tel. 800-826-4180. North of Sedona in Boynton Canyon: 525 Boynton Canyon Road. 162 rooms.

L'Auberge de Sedona $$$
Luxury and seclusion are the hallmarks of this hotel, a French country lodge and cabins located along the banks of Oak Creek in a **setting of dramatic natural beauty**. You are conveniently located right in the heart of town, but you feel miles away once you drop down to the property. The gorgeous natural landscape will captivate you. All the **guestrooms are large** and beautifully furnished. **Two gourmet restaurants** are a treat in themselves. The heated pool and hot tub are great spots to soak in the views. *Info*: www.lauberge.com. Tel. 800-272-6777. Downtown Sedona: 301 L'Auberge Lane. 67 rooms.

More of Sedona's Best

Sedona

There are so many excellent high-end resorts in Sedona it's hard to go wrong with any of them. In addition to the two listed above, you can try the wonderfully spacious Adobe Grand Villas (www.adobegrandvillas.com, Tel. 866-900-7616) or the smooth and refined Amara Creekside Resort (www.amararesort.com, Tel. 866.455.6610.)

Sedona Rouge $$
The hip entry in the hotel market, the décor of the Sedona Rouge conjures up images of the Mediterranean and North Africa. Converting a standard motel into a **chic destination** is not easy, but these guys have pulled it off. Rooms feature **flatscreen TVs and wireless internet**. Full range of spa treatments available. **Excellent dining** at Reds. *Info*: www.sedonarouge.com. Tel. 866-312-4111. West of downtown: 2250 West Hwy 89A. 77 rooms.

Sky Ranch Lodge $$
A great value, this motel-style property is located **away from the hustle and bustle of town atop a mesa** that affords **spectacular views**. Brilliant by sun-filled day, the view takes on a special warmth in the evening as the lights of Sedona twinkle in the fading daylight. Both the grounds and the rooms are spacious and comfortable. Some rooms include kitchenettes. Pool and hot tub. Info: www.skyranchlodge.com. Tel. 888-708-6400. In town near the airport: Top of Airport Road. 94 rooms.

Bell Rock Inn $
A nice value in the moderately priced category, the Bell Rock Inn is attractive and comfortable. **Within a few steps of red rock formations** – they almost look like they are touching the building as you gaze over the rooftops. The name of the hotel comes from the nearby Bell Rock, which is an excellent hike. Many of the rooms are **mini-suites with fireplaces**. Two heated swimming pools and a hot tub. *Info*: www.ilxresorts.com. Tel. 800-881-7625. Five miles south of downtown in the village of Oak Creek: 6246 Highway 179. 96 rooms.

SEDONA BEST EATS
L'Auberge Restaurant at L'Auberge de Sedona $$$
This romantic spot, tucked in near the gurgling Oak Creek, is pretty much the **epitome of perfection**. With **impeccable French cuisine** and service, L'Auberge really treats you like royalty. The **patio** just might be the most exquisite spot in Sedona. If you can't afford dinner, try the wonderful breakfast here. Dress pants and collared shirts for men. *Info*: Tel. 928-282-1667. Downtown: 301 L'Auberge Lane. Open daily for breakfast, lunch, and dinner. Dinner reservations recommended.

Yavapai at Enchantment Resort $$$
Given the **amazing views of Boynton Canyon** offered here, the restaurant would be packed regardless of the quality of food. They take it a step further though and offer **world-class cuisine** to go with the world-class vistas. Featuring seasonal fresh ingredients and an extensive wine list, this is a special place. Dress pants and collared shirts for men. *Info*: Tel. 928-204-6000. North of town: 525 Boynton Canyon Rd. Open daily for breakfast, lunch, and dinner. Dinner reservations recommended.

El Rincon Restaurante Mexicano $$
Featuring **Mexican cuisine with a bit of Navajo influence**, El Rincon has been a Sedona standard for 30 years. Located in the pleasant "village" of Tlaquepaque, El Rincon's décor fits right in. The adobe building features tile and iron work from Mexico. Try the **Navajo pizzas** if you aren't going to make it up to the Navajo Nation. *Info*: Tel. 928-282-4648. Located just south of the Y on

Hwy. 179 at The Bridge. Open daily 11am-9pm (8pm on Sundays.) Dinner reservations recommended.

Oaxaca Mexican Restaurant $$
Oaxaca, right in the center of downtown, is a perennial favorite with both locals and visitors. The **patio seating offers fantastic views**. Unlike many Mexican restaurants, there are actually **quite a few healthy options** on the menu. (Although who can resist a big plate of cheesy enchiladas?) Nice tequila selection too. *Info*: Tel. 928-282-6291. Downtown: 321 Hwy 89A. Open 8am-9pm.

Reds Bistro at Sedona Rouge $$
Stylish and chic, Reds manages to pull off being comfortable at the same time. The food, **haute takes on many American favorites**, is absolutely delicious. Enjoy the upscale atmosphere of the dining room, or just relax in the contemporary bar area. *Info*: Tel. 928-203-4111. West of downtown: 2250 West Hwy 89A. Open daily breakfast, lunch, and dinner daily.

Sedona Airport Restaurant $$
Yes, eating at the airport is a little random, but in Sedona it means **great views and good food** at the same time. Be advised that **breakfast is served until noon** and it's not a place to go if you're in a hurry. *Info*: Tel. 928-282-3576. In town at the airport: 1185 Airport Rd. Open daily 7am-8:30pm.

Desert Flour Bakery & Bistro $
Stop in for **sinfully delicious pastries**, or grab one of their **excellent made-to-order sandwiches**. You can eat in, or take your food along for a picnic. The salads here are also outstanding. *Info*: Tel. 928-284-4633. South of downtown in the Village of Oak Creek. 6446 Highway 179. Open 7am-3pm Monday,Tuesday. 7am-8:30pm Wednesday-Saturday. 8am - 2pm Sundays.

Sedona Coffee Roasters $
Serving coffee, baked goods, and deli sandwiches, the Sedona Coffee Roasters is a great place to grab and go or sit and sip a while. *Info*: Tel. 928-282-0282. West of downtown: 2155 W Highway 89A #118. Open 7am-5pm daily.

GRAND CANYON BEST SLEEPS

SOUTH RIM BEST SLEEPS
Xanterra Parks & Resorts, who have operations in many of the country's national parks, manage all of the hotels on the South Rim. There is **one central reservations number** (Tel. 888-297-2757) and **one reservations website** (www.grandcanyonlodges.com.) They handle reservations for all hotel and dining on the South Rim. For same day reservations call Tel. 928-638-2631.

The Grand Canyon is very popular so please **make your reservations well in advance**. If you can't get lodging in the park, **Tusayan** has some hotels and is within "commuting" distance of the Grand Canyon. Be sure to call and **check on last-minute availability** if you haven't been able to reserve your dream choice. One time in the winter I was even able to get walk-up reservations at Phantom Ranch.

El Tovar Hotel $$
The first hotel to be built at the Grand Canyon, this wonderful establishment was **built in 1905** and most recently renovated in 2005. The architectural style, known as "rustic", aimed to create a structure that complemented its surroundings. You'll see **native stone and massive pine logs** throughout the building. Guestrooms range from small to very large, but are all nicely furnished. Some have **amazing canyon views**. The restaurant is outstanding. On the canyon rim. *Info*: Tel. 888-297-2757. www.grandcanyonlodges.com. Grand Canyon Village. 78 rooms.

Kachina and Thunderbird Lodges $$
These sister properties are nearly **identical in appearance and facilities** and are literally connected. You can't really tell them apart. The rooms are simple, **like a modern motel**, but comfortable. The **location however, is awesome**. You are within walking distance of all the facilities of the Grand Canyon Village. Some rooms have canyon views. On the canyon rim. *Info*: Tel. 888-297-2757. www.grandcanyonlodges.com. Grand Canyon Village. 49 and 55 rooms respectively.

Bright Angel Lodge $-$$

Built in 1935, the Bright Angel is **one of the park's most historic properties**. Designed by famous architect Mary J. Colter, the rustic style is more simple that than of El Tovar. Like the former, however, it features an **attractive and comfortable lobby with a massive fireplace**. The rooms are either in the main building or in small cabins. Eleven of the rooms do not have private bath, but some larger rooms have fireplaces and canyon views. On the canyon rim. Restaurant and lounge. *Info*: Tel. 888-297-2757. www.grandcanyonlodges.com. Grand Canyon Village. 88 rooms.

Grand Canyon

Yavapai Lodge $-$$

Nestled amid a forest of pinon and juniper trees, Yavapai is the **largest hotel in the park**. The motel-style rooms are very similar to those of Maswik. There are no views, but you have the convenience of staying in the park. Cafeteria and mini-mart. *Info*: Tel. 888-297-2757. www.grandcanyonlodges.com. One mile from Grand Canyon Village. 358 rooms.

Maswik Lodge $

This **modern lodge**, with motel style rooms, is spread out over several acres of ponderosa pine. (The north rooms are the largest.) There are also **cabins available in the summer**. The biggest benefit is that you are **close to the Grand Canyon Village and rim**. Cafeteria and lounge. *Info*: Tel. 888-297-2757. www.grandcanyonlodges.com. One quarter mile from Grand Canyon Village. 248 rooms.

Phantom Ranch $

If you want to **spend the night on the canyon floor** and don't want to camp, this is your only option. Located alongside Bright Angel Creek, Phantom Ranch was **constructed in 1922 of uncut boulders** taken from the Colorado River. Cabins are available for those taking the two-night mule trip. The other accommodations consist of **men's and women's dormitories**. The food, which you must reserve before you descend, is delicious. *Info*: Tel. 888-297-2757. www.grandcanyonlodges.com. Canyon floor. 11 cabins. 10 bunk beds in each dormitory.

Desert View Campground $
50 first-come, first-serve sites that offer wonderful canyon views and impressive sunrises. Tel. 928-638-7888.

Grand Canyon Suites $$
This hotel is not in the Grand Canyon, but rather just outside the park in Tusayan. This is only a good option if you can't get lodging in the park. They do have a little more space to spread out as well as microwaves and refrigerators. *Info*: Tel. 888-538-5353. One block west of AZ-64 in Tusayan. 34 rooms.

More Tusayan Options

If you can't get a room in the park or at the Grand Canyon Suites, try the national chains. Both Holiday Inn Express (Tel. 800-315-2621, www. Holidayinn.com) and Best Western (Tel. 800-780-7234, www.bestwestern.com) have properties in Tusayan.

Ten-X Campground $
70 first-come, first-serve sites in the woods just south of the park entrance. *Info*: Tel. 928-638-2443.

GRAND CANYON BEST EATS

SOUTH RIM BEST EATS
El Tover Dining Room $$-$$$
Considering the informality of the Grand Canyon, you will be surprised at the **formal nature of the dining experience** at the El Tovar Dining Room. Although patrons are all dressed in hiking clothes, the servers are decked out in tuxedo shirts. If you can get reservations **you should not miss dinner here**. The room is spacious and attractive and the **food is gourmet**. Picture windows provide excellent views while you wait for your food. Excellent wine list. *Info*: Tel. 888-297-2757. El Tovar Hotel in the Grand Canyon Village. Open for breakfast, lunch, and dinner daily. Reservations suggested.

Arizona Room $$
Located near the Bright Angel Lodge, the Arizona Room offers

up tender, sizzling steaks. There are also chicken and fish dishes as well as salad. Here too, windows face the canyon. Cocktails and wine are served. *Info*: Tel. 888-297-2757. Grand Canyon Village. Open for breakfast, lunch, and dinner daily.

Bright Angel Dining Room $

A **more casual experience** than the El Tovar dining room, this restaurant features an ample selection of dishes including several vegetarian offerings. Service is friendly and efficient. Cocktails and wine are served. *Info*: Tel. 888-297-2757. Bright Angel Lodge in the Grand Canyon Village. Open for breakfast, lunch, and dinner daily.

SOUTH RIM TO NORTH RIM DRIVING ROUTE
BEST SLEEPS & EATS

Cameron Trading Post Hotel $-$$

Located at the historic Cameron Trading Post, the lodge offers comfortable rooms decorated in a southwestern motif. With **views of the Little Colorado River Gorge**, this is a good spot if you find yourself between the South and North Rims in the evening. **Pleasant garden and good restaurant** as well. *Info*: Tel. 800-338-7385. www.camerontradingpost.com. Just north of Cameron. 66 rooms.

Cameron Trading Post Dining Room $

The Cameron Trading Post would be worth a stop for a meal simply for the **views of the Little Colorado River Gorge** and the architecture of the dining room (the pressed tin ceiling is especially notable.) Luckily the food is good as well. Go for the Southwestern and **Navajo-influenced dishes**. *Info*: Tel. 800-338-7385. Just north of Cameron. Open for breakfast, lunch, and dinner daily.

Marble Canyon Lodge Dining Room $

Basic coffee shop and dining room **in the middle of nowhere**. Good place to stop en route. *Info*: Tel. 928-355-2225. Immediately north of the Navajo Bridge on US-89A. Open for breakfast, lunch, and dinner daily

NORTH RIM BEST SLEEPS & EATS
Grand Canyon Lodge $-$$
This is a wonderful place to stay because of the **unparalleled natural setting** and the charming accommodations. There are both motel-style room and cabins rooms, but the outstanding cabins rooms facing the rim should be your first choice. The main building was constructed of limestone and massive timber beams in the 1930s. The **outside verandas have one of the most beautiful views of the canyon** found anywhere in the park. The restaurant is also excellent. Closed October-May. *Info*: Tel. 888-297-2757. Same day reservations 928-638-2611. www.grandcanyonnorthrim.com. On the rim. 165 cabins and 40 rooms.

North Rim Campground $
Eighty-six sites, some reservable, on the rim facing the canyon. Great for sunset. *Info*: Tel. 800-365-2267.

Grand Canyon Lodge Dining Room $-$$
Like the lodge in which it is located, the dining room is a spacious facility with high timbered ceiling beams and **simply breathtaking views of the canyon from two different directions**. The service is quick and efficient. The selection of food is somewhat limited but nicely prepared. Cocktails available. *Info*: Tel. 888-297-2757. Same day reservations 928-638-2611. Open for breakfast, lunch, and dinner daily. Reservations recommended for dinner.

North Rim Alternatives

If you can't get a reservation at the North Rim, you can head for Jacob Lake, 45 miles away. Try the **Jacob Lake Inn** (Tel. 928-643-7232, www.jacoblake.com) or the first-come, first-serve **Jacob Lake Campground** (Tel. 928-643-7395.)

OFF THE BEATEN PATH BEST SLEEPS & EATS
Havasu Falls – Havasupai Lodge $$
The lodge here is simple, but after the eight-mile hike down it's **a welcome sight**. There is a café here in Supai as well. *Info*: Tel. 928-448-2111. www.kaibab.org/supai. In the village of Supai.

Havasu Campground $
Located near the falls, reservations are required. *Info*: Tel. 928-448-2141.

Grand Canyon West - Hualapai Lodge $
The rooms here are **pretty basic**, but they are clean and comfortable which is all you can really hope for. The accompanying **Diamond Creek Restaurant** serves up hearty plates of food. Good stop-over place for the one-day rafting trips. *Info*: Tel. 888-255-9550. www.grandcanyonresort.com. Peach Springs, Arizona.

NORTHEASTERN ARIZONA BEST SLEEPS & EATS

CANYON DE CHELLY/CHINLE BEST SLEEPS & EATS
Holiday Inn $$
Just a half-mile from the park entrance, this Holiday Inn is located at was once Garcia's Trading Post. That gives it much **more charm than you would usually get from a chain hotel**. It has a few more amenities than the Thunderbird lodge, like an **outdoor pool** and high-speed internet. The restaurant is good as well. Canyon tours available. *Info*: Tel. 800-315-2621. www.holidayinn.com. Half-mile from the entrance to Canyon de Chelly. Indian Route 7 - Garcia Trading Post. 108 rooms.

Thunderbird Lodge $-$$
Not only does the Thunderbird Lodge provide the **convenience** of staying right in Canyon de Chelly National Monument, it is also a very pleasant and attractive facility. It is not within sight of the canyon (even though it's only seven hundred yards from the beginning of it), but it is **surrounded by a large grove of beautiful cottonwood trees**. There are two sections of the lodge – the older rooms are smaller but you really can't go wrong in either section. The cafeteria style restaurant is surprising good. Operated by the Navajo Nation. Canyon tours available. *Info*: Tel. 800-679-2473. www.tbirdlodge.com. In Canyon de Chelly National Monument. 72 rooms.

If these two hotels are full, there is a decent **Best Western in Chinle**, which is only two miles from the park. (Tel. 800-780-7234, www.bestwestern.com)

Garcia's at the Holiday Inn $
The only table-served restaurant near the park, Garcia's is a **good bet after a long day of touring**. The homemade bread is quite

Canyon de
Chelly-
Chinle
good although you'll have to ask for more kick in the southwestern dishes if you like spicy food. *Info*: Tel. 800-315-2621. One half
mile outside the entrance to Canyon del Chelly: Indian Route 7 -
Garcia Trading Post. Open for breakfast, lunch and dinner daily.

Hopi Mesas

Lake Powell
Thunderbird Lodge Dining Room $
This multi-room dining facility offers a good variety of American, Southwestern, and Native American food. It is served café
style, but is still **excellent**. The restaurant is **located in the
original trading post** and in the center is a vault-like room that
once served at as jail. Beautiful Navajo rugs and other crafts
decorate the walls. *Info*: Tel. 800-679-2473. In Canyon de Chelly
National Monument. Open daily for breakfast, lunch and dinner.

HOPI MESAS BEST SLEEPS & EATS
Hopi Cultural Center Motel $
Very **simple motel-style rooms**, but the only place to stay in the
mesas. There is a restaurant here as well as a museum. *Info*: Tel.
928-734-2401. www.psv.com/hopi.html. Second Mesa. 33 rooms.

Hopi Cultural Center Restaurant $
Run by the Hopi people, this restaurant **offers many authentic
Hopi dishes**. *Info*: Tel. 928-734-2401. Second Mesa. Open daily for
breakfast, lunch, and dinner.

LAKE POWELL BEST SLEEPS
Lake Powell Resort $$-$$$
Spread out on the shoreline of magnificent Lake Powell, the
setting of this resort makes it worth a stay. The two-story motor
inn type buildings feature rooms that are reasonable attractive
and comfortable. All have a patio or balcony, but those that face
the lake have the best views. Amenities include two heated
swimming pools and a workout area. This is also the place for
boat rentals and boat tours, so staying here makes it that much
more convenient. The dining room is nice although a bit expensive, but there is also a pizza restaurant on site. *Info*: Tel. 800-528-
6154. www.lakepowell.com. Four miles north of Page on the
shores of Lake Powell: 100 Lakeshore Dr. 350 rooms.

Best Western Arizonainn $-$$

Yes, the spelling is correct – no space between Arizona and inn. This attractive motel is located at the top of a hill that **overlooks Lake Powell and the Glen Canyon Dam**. If your room faces in that direction then you're in for a special treat. It's definitely worth spending a few dollars more for the vistas. The location is convenient for activities on both the lake and in town. Heated swimming pool, restaurant, and free continental breakfast. *Info*: Tel. 800-826-2718. www.bestwestern.com. 716 Rimview Drive. 103 rooms.

Lake Powell Days Inn & Suites $-$$

One of the newest hotels in town, this is a **good choice for families** as there are 22 suites that not only include a separate living space with a sofa bed, but also microwaves and refrigerators. The pool is a pleasant place to cool off after a day of adventuring. Nice views of Lake Powell. Breakfast included. Info: Tel. 877-525-3769. www.daysinn.net. In Page: 961 N US 89. 82 rooms.

LAKE POWELL BEST EATS
Bella Napoli $

Bella Napoli is best known and loved locally for their **excellent pizza**. Beer and wine are served, as are other Italian entrees. *Info*: Tel. 928-645-2706. 810 N Navajo Dr. Dinner served nightly.

Dam Bar & Grille $

Decked out in the full "dam" theme, including hard hats on the concrete walls, this restaurant is definitely part of the Page scene. **Great prime rib**, but also yummy burgers and salads. *Info*: Tel: 928-645-2161. 644 N Navajo Dr.

Zapatas Great Mexican Food $

This popular restaurant serves up **good food in a fun atmosphere**. Popular with locals for both lunch and dinner, so consider making a reservation. With live music on some nights and tasty drinks, this is a nice place to linger. *Info*: Tel. 928-645-9006. 615 N Navajo Dr. Open daily 11am-10pm. Reservation recommended.

MONUMENT VALLEY BEST SLEEPS & EATS

Monument Valley

Greer

Goulding's Lodge $-$$
Although technically located in Utah, Goulding's Lodge is very much a part of the Monument Valley environs and the closest hotel to the park. The accommodations are pretty basic motel-style rooms, but they **all have balconies with wonderful views** of Monument Valley. Be sure to **ask if any of the three houses are available**. They cost the same as hotel rooms and offer full kitchens and fireplaces. **House #340** has one of the most amazing views you'll ever experience anywhere. Many film crews and stars have stayed here over the years. Good restaurant. Tours available. Pool and wireless internet. *Info*: Tel. 435-727-3231. www.gouldings.com. Monument Valley, UT. 62 rooms. 3 houses.

If you can't get a room at Gouldings, **Kayenta**, 25-miles south, is the closest town with lodging. The best choices there are the **Hampton Inn** (Tel. 800-426-7866. www.hamptoninn.com) and the **Holiday Inn** (Tel. **800-315-2621**. www.holidayinn.com)

Stagecoach Dining Room at Goulding's Lodge $
The dining room at Goulding's offers wonderful looks at Monument Valley. You'll enjoy sitting in front of the view windows eating **Navajo-influenced dishes**. *Info*: Tel. 435-727-3231. Monument Valley, UT. Open daily for breakfast, lunch and dinner.

EASTERN ARIZONA BEST SLEEPS & EATS

GREER BEST SLEEPS
Red Setter Inn $$-$$$
A beautiful property on the banks of the Little Colorado, this inn does everything right. With ten acres of pine, fir, spruce and aspen trees, as well as a private stretch of the river, this is a place for peace and tranquility. (No children under 16 are allowed.) The cottage and guestrooms feature wonderful down comforters and fireplaces. Cookies await every afternoon. Delightful porch overlooking the river. *Info*: www.redsetterinn.com. Tel. 888-994-7337. #8 Main Street. 12 rooms.

X-Diamond Ranch $$

A **working ranch** since the early 1900s, the X-Diamond offers something for everybody. **Horseback riding** is one of the favorite activities, but you can also hike, fish, and even **participate in an archeological dig** on the ranch's own ruin site. Six large and comfortable cabins, with walking distance of the Little Colorado River, are more like nice houses. Plenty of elk and deer roaming around through the pines. *Info*: www.xdiamondranch.com. Tel. 928-333-2286. East of Greer off of AZ-260. 6 cabins.

Greer

Greer Lodge Resort $-$$

This resort features rooms inside the main lodge (no children under 16) and multiple cabins spread around the property as well as across Main Street. The accommodations are all comfortable but basic. The **cabins are a good bet for families**. The grounds include a **wonderful meadow with multiple curving sections of the Little Colorado River** as well as three ponds. (All great for fishing.) Good restaurant and lounge and even occasional barn dances. *Info*: www.greerlodgeaz.com. Tel. 928-735-7216. 44 Main Street. 10 guestrooms, 25 cabins.

Gourmet Guest Ranch!

For a guest ranch experience that includes gourmet meals and luxury accommodations, try **Hidden Meadow Ranch**. (www.hiddenmeadowranch.com. Tel. 866-333-4080) Depending on their capacity, they also accept some reservations for lunch, dinner, and Saturday brunch if you are staying elsewhere. The meal will be well-worth the trip if it fits in your budget.

Molly Butler Lodge $

In business since the early 1900s, the Molly Butler Lodge is a simple, rustic place that makes you feel right at home. The restaurant serves good country-style meals, while the lounge is a fun place to spend an evening shooting pool and feeding the juke box. *Info*: www.mollybutlerlodge.com. Tel. 866-288-3167. 109 Main Street. 11 rooms.

GREER BEST EATS

373 Grill at the Greer Lodge Resort $-$$

With a comfortable lodge atmosphere, the 373 Grill offers a **menu** that will make everybody happy. From steaks and salmon to salads and burgers. Pleasant multi-level decks overlook the Little Colorado River. *Info*: Tel. 928-735-7216. 44 N. Main St. Open daily breakfast, lunch and dinner.

Amberian Peaks Lodge and Restaurant $
While the dining room here is nice, the best thing about Amberian Peaks is the take-out pizza. Even though many cabins in the area come with kitchens, sometimes you don't want to cook. Call the Peaks and you're taken care of. *Info*: Tel. 928-735-9977. 1 Main Street. Call to see if serving as hours vary depending on the season.

Rendezvous Diner $
Housed in what was once Greer's main post office, this diner is now a wonderful spot for home-cooking and tasty desserts. The small restaurant features friendly staff in a very informal atmosphere. Ask about pie specials and be sure to order them *ala mode*. *Info*: Tel. 928-735-7483. 117 Main Street. Open daily breakfast, lunch and dinner.

HANNAGAN MEADOW BEST SLEEPS & EATS
Hannagan Meadow Lodge $-$$
While the accommodations and dining are pretty simple here, the location is out of this world. Situated at 9100 feet in the Apache-Sitgreaves National Forest, Hannagan Meadow is a wonderful getaway. If you love outdoor activities, you'll be in heaven here. Photographers come for the wildlife…birds, elk, coyotes, deer and even wolves. The cabins are equipped with kitchens and the lodge rooms include breakfast. The home-style restaurant is open for certain meals only, depending on the season. There is also a general store that offers basic grocery items, snacks and drinks. *Info*: www.hannaganmeadow.com. Tel. 928-339-4370. 22 miles south of Alpine on the Coronado Trail (US 191). 7 lodge rooms. 10 cabins.

PAYSON BEST SLEEPS & EATS
Kohl's Ranch Lodge $$-$$$
This delightful forest-surrounded lodge almost qualifies as a guest ranch. Types of accommodations include motel-type bed-

rooms, multi-bedroom units, and several large cabins. **Some include full kitchens**. The **recreational facilities are extensive and impressive** — heated swimming pool, sauna, whirlpool, exercise room, sports court, horseshoes, bocciball, and golf. There are hiking and jogging trails in the surrounding woods. Biking and horseback riding can also be arranged. *Info*: www.kohlsranch.com. Tel. 800-521-3131. East Highway 260. 49 rooms.

The Oaks Restaurant $$
Excellent food served in a warm and friendly atmosphere. **Dine outside on the patio** in the summer surrounded by the scent of pine. Prime rib, steaks, and seafood all expertly prepared to your order. Popular Sunday brunch. *Info*: Tel. 928-474-1929. 302 West Main. Open for lunch and dinner daily. Reservations recommended during summer.

PINETOP-LAKESIDE BEST SLEEPS & EATS
Whispering Pines Resort $-$$
Great location **secluded in the pines on 12 acres** of land bordering National Forest. The simple but **comfortable cabins** come in studio, one, two, and three and bedroom configurations. All come stocked with wood for the fireplace. There are **paths to both Woodland Lake and Walnut Creek** from the property. Quiet and peaceful yet also family friendly with a playground for kids. *Info*: www.whiperingpinesaz.com. Tel. 800-840-3867. AZ-260, just beyond mile marker 352, Pinetop. 35 cabins.

Woodland Inn and Suites $
With **clean, affordable rooms**, this is a good option for those on a budget. All rooms come with refrigerators and breakfast is included. A **very friendly staff** makes for a pleasant experience. *Info*: www.shiloinns.com/Arizona/woodlandsuite.html. Tel. 800-222-2244. 458 E. White Mountain Blvd, Pinetop. 42 rooms.

Charlie Clark's Steakhouse $$
A fun and casual place for a real western dinner. The building looks like a frontier cabin in the woods. Choose from a host of hearty fare that includes delicious slow cooked prime rib, rotisserie chicken, and mesquite steaks grilled to perfection. The atmosphere and food appeal to both children and adults. *Info*:

Tel. 928-367-4900. 1701 E White Mountain Blvd, Pinetop. Open nightly. Reservations recommended.

Christmas Tree Restaurant $$
No matter what time of year you eat here, there's a bit of December in the air as the restaurant is fully decked out for Christmas year-round. Highlights are the freshly baked cinnamon rolls as well as the chicken and dumplings. *Info*: Tel. 928-367-3107. 455 N Woodland Road, Lakeside. Open for dinner nightly except Tuesday. Reservations recommended.

WINSLOW BEST SLEEPS & EATS
La Posada Hotel $$
Back in the day when travel by railroad was the best way to go, elegant hotels were built along the route to continue that first class experience after travelers left the rail. La Posada, a **hacienda designed by famous architect Mary Colter** (who also designed many Grand Canyon buildings), is one of these hotels. Recently restored to its **1930s grandeur**, La Posada is a wonderful place to spend a day or two. The rooms, decorated with period pieces, are delightful spots to sit and look out at the garden or passing trains. No phones in rooms, although they do have cable TV. The Turquoise Room **restaurant is worth a stop** even if you're not spending the night. *Info*: www.laposada.org. Tel. 928-289-4366. 303 E. Second Street (Route 66). 38 rooms.

Turquoise Room at La Posada Hotel $$$
The Santa Fe Railroad's Super Chief was so luxurious that it became the favorite train of celebrities traveling across country. The "Train of the Stars" had an unmatched private dining car called the Turquoise Room. Recreating that type of elegant dining experience, this restaurant offers fantastic fare in a wonderful setting. The **Route 66 Cadillac Margarita is a splended start to any meal and goes well with the pork carnitas.** *Info*: Tel 928-289-4366. 303 E. Second Street (Route 66). Open daily breakfast, lunch, and dinner. Dinner reservations recommended.

WESTERN ARIZONA BEST SLEEPS & EATS

KINGMAN BEST SLEEPS & EATS
Hotel Brunswick $-$$
Charming and comfortable, this is the perfect place to stay if you want to experience historic Kingman. The rooms are on the smaller side, but the hotel has real allure. Go for a suite if you need more space. Be warned that many trains pass by every night, but they hand out earplugs at check-in. *Info*: www.hotel-brunswick.com. Tel. 928-718-1800. 315 East Andy Devine. 24 rooms.

Hualapai Mountain Park Cabins $
These rustic cabins offer the wonderful chance for a high-mountain getaway very near Kingman. Some come with fireplaces or wood burning stoves. *Info*: www.mcparks.com/hmp. Hualapai Mountain Park, 6230 Hualapai Mountain Road. Tel. (877) 757-0915. 16 cabins.

Dambar & Steakhouse $-$$
Although thick and **juicy steaks** are the main attraction at Dambar, the menu has a wide variety of items including sandwiches and salads. Friendly and efficient service. **Popular with locals**, so you might have to wait a bit on weekends. *Info*: Tel. 928-753-3253. 1960 E Andy Devine. Lunch and dinner daily.

Hubb's Bistro in the Hotel Brunswick $-$$
Eating at Hubb's, which offers American fare like burgers and sandwiches, **is a must** even if you're not staying at the Hotel Brunswick. The **historic atmosphere** is priceless. There are also a few French dishes on the menu as the proprietor Gerard is from the other side of the pond. Mulligan's Bar is also worth a stop for a drink. *Info*: Tel. 928-718-1800. 315 East Andy Devine. Closed Sunday.

LAKE HAVASU BEST SLEEPS & EATS
London Bridge Resort $$-$$$
A most **attractive waterfront resort**, it is part of the complex that contains the London Bridge and the shopping village. The rooms

Lake
Havasu
Wickenburg
Yuma

are actually studio, one bedroom, and two bedroom suites. Some have **excellent lake views**. Recreational facilities include swimming pools, spa, tennis, and golf as well as **every water sport imaginable**. Private sandy beach. Two restaurants and a cocktail lounge. *Info*: Tel. 866-331-9231. www.londonbridgeresort.com. In the center of town on Thompson Bay. 1477 Queen's Bay Road. 122 suites.

Sands Vacation Resort $-$$
Another **all-suite facility** featuring either one or two bedroom apartments with full kitchens. The suites are spacious and comfortable with a separate living area. **Heated pool, tennis court, horseshoes, and bocce.** *Info*: Tel. 800-521-0360. www.sands-resort.com. One mile from bridge at 2040 Mesquite Ave. 42 suites.

Martini Bay Lounge & Restaurant $$
Located inside the London Bridge Resort, Martini Bay has excellent outdoor seating on multiple verandas and patios. Specializing in tapas, little dishes from Spain that are meant to be ordered by the plateful and shared, Martini Bay has created a fun atmosphere and serves good food. Martinis, of course, are the house specialty. *Info*: Tel. 928-855-0888. www.londonbridgeresort.com. In the center of town on Thompson Bay. 1477 Queen's Bay Road. Dinner served Tuesday-Saturday starting at 4pm.

Mudshark Brewing Company $-$$
With great pizza and burgers, friendly service, and **tasty beers to sample**, the Mudshark is a favorite for locals and visitors alike. Try the Scorpion Amber Ale with the Mushroom Swiss Burger and you'll go home happy for sure. *Info*: Tel. 928-453-2981. 210 Swanson Ave. Open for lunch and dinner daily.

WICKENBURG BEST SLEEPS & EATS
See the **Western Arizona** chapter for information on Wickenburg's **outstanding guest ranches**. They all offer full-meal plans.

YUMA BEST SLEEPS & EATS
La Fuente Inn & Suites $-$$
With spacious and attractive grounds, La Fuente is an oasis in the desert. The building's architecture is Spanish style and the front

entrance features a large fountain with water tumbling down a series of boulders. The inner courtyard has well manicured lawns bordered by trees and shrubs that enclose the swimming pool and pretty gazebo. The rooms are simply but thoughtfully furnished. Facilities include a heated pool, whirlpool, and exercise room. There is no restaurant, but a continental breakfast is included as are evening complimentary beverages. *Info*: www.lafuenteinn.com. Tel. 800-841-1814. 1513 East 16th St. 96 rooms.

Yuma

El Pappagallo Mexican Restaurant $-$$
Great Mexican food served by very nice people. Try the huevos rancheros or carne asada. The salsa is made fresh daily. *Info*: Tel. 928-343-9451. 1401 S Avenue B. Open daily 11am-9pm.

12. BEST ACTIVITIES

This chapter covers Arizona's best vacation activities: shopping, nightlife, and year-round sports and recreation. You'll find great stores unique to Arizona, Indian casinos, fun bars and nightclubs, dance joints, and suggestions for breathtaking hikes, raft and float trips, ballooning, golf, tennis, biking, skiing, and much more!

PHOENIX-SCOTTSDALE BEST SHOPPING

There are malls all over Phoenix, but a few deserve special mention. They offer not only shopping, but also excellent dining and even nightlife choices. The most impressive is **Scottsdale Fashion Square** (www.fasionsquare.com) near Old Town Scottsdale at Camelback and Scottsdale Road. With over 225 retailers, including Nordstrom and Neiman Marcus, it's the largest mall in the southwest.

If you are near the Camelback Corridor and are in need of a little retail therapy, try **Biltmore Fashion Park** at Camelback and 24th

St. (www.shopbiltmore.com) With an open-air park setting, you can enjoy the weather while you shop.

If you're in North Scottsdale you can enjoy **Kierland Commons,** a "main street" shopping experience at Scottsdale Road and Greenway (www.kierlandcommons.com). Set up to mimic the tranquility of walking from store to store in a little town, Kierland is centered around a central square and fountain.

For **specialty shops and unique boutiques,** Scottsdale is tops. **The Borgata,** at Scottsdale Road and Lincoln, offers many one-of-a-kind stores, as does **Old Town Scottsdale** itself, especially on 5th Ave. Don't overlook the **museum gift stores** at the Heard, Phoenix Art Museum and Scottsdale Museum of Contemporary Art for some great finds.

Popular **resale stores** include **My Sisters Closet** (www.mysisterscloset.com), with locations in Scottsdale and the Camelback Corridor, for **high-end items.** Look to **Buffalo Exchange** in Tempe for more **campus-oriented** styles. (www.buffaloexchange.com)

Old Town Scottsdale is also the place to shop for **Native American** as well as **Western items.** The area just east of Scottsdale Road and south of Indian School has many stores that fit this bill. Try **Atkinson's Trading Post** on Brown, and **Gilbert Ortega Galleries** on East 5th Ave.

PHOENIX-SCOTTSDALE BEST NIGHTLIFE

While the hot spots constantly change, their general locations tend to stay more or less the same. The hopping **Scottsdale** nightlife can generally be found in **Old Town.** Perennial favorites include the double clubs at **Axis/Radius** (www.axis-radius.com) and the **Martini Ranch** (www.martiniranchaz.com.). The hotel lobby bars at the "hip" hotels are also well worth a visit. Try **The Bar** at the Mondrian Hotel, the **Zuzu Lounge** at the Valley Ho, or the **Jade Bar** at the Sanctuary Resort. The lobby bar at the **Hyatt Gainey** is fantastic for casual drinks outside. The **Kazbar,** a

speakeasy with an unmarked door on Stetson, is a must for late-
night drinks and live music. (www.kazbar.net.) If you want to
experience a full-on country bar, don't miss the **Rusty Spur
Saloon** (www.rustyspursaloon.com) on Main St.

Downtown Phoenix is home to plenty of bars capitalizing on
their **proximity to major professional sports** teams. Try **Dan
Majerle's Sports Grill** (www.majerles.com) for hoops and happy
hour or **Alice Cooper'stown** (www.alicecooperstown.com) where
jocks and rock meet. The ambiance at the **Bar Bianco** on Heritage
Square is a sure hit as well. (www.pizzeriabianco.com)

If **gambling** is your pleasure, you won't have to drive far in the
Valley to find a **casino**. The best and largest is **Casino Arizona** at
101 and McKellips just south of Scottsdale. They also have a
smaller satellite location at 101 and Indian Bend that is more
convenient to many Scottsdale hotels (www.casinoaz.com). Other
casinos can be found in Fountain Hills, in Gilbert, and also
Apache Junction.

If you'd like to find time for a little culture at night, there are a
number of excellent locations for the **performing arts**. Check
websites before you visit for up-to-date information. The biggies
include the **Gammage Auditorium** at ASU in Tempe
(www.asugammage.com), the **Herberger Theater Center** in Phoenix (www.herbergertheater.org), the **Scottsdale Center for the
Performing Arts** (www.scottsdaleperformingarts.org), and the
new kid on the block, the amazing **Mesa Arts Center**
(www.mesaartscenter.com.)

PHOENIX-SCOTTSDALE BEST SPORTS & RECREATION

Spectator Sports
Baseball
There's always something happening sports-wise in the Valley.
Perhaps the biggest draw is the Cactus League, **Major League
spring training** games that blanket the Phoenix metropolitan
area in March. (www.cactus-league.com)

Once the baseball season begins in earnest, you can enjoy the **Arizona Diamondbacks** at Chase Field in downtown Phoenix. The great thing is they **close the roof and pump in AC** when the temperatures rise. (http://arizona.diamondbacks.mlb.com) At the college level, the ASU baseball team is a perennial power-house.

Other profession teams in the Valley include the **Phoenix Suns**, who play **basketball** in downtown Phoenix at the **US Airways Center** (www.nba.com/suns); the **Arizona Cardinals**, with their new high tech **football** stadium in **Glendale** (www.azcardinals.com); and the **Phoenix Coyotes** of the National **Hockey** League who play in **Glendale** also (www.phoenixcoyotes.com). On the women's side there is **the Phoenix Mercury basketball** team who plan in the US Airways Center (www.wnba.com/mercury). Additional teams include the **Arizona Sting lacrosse** team (www.arizonasting.com) and the **Arizona Rattlers Arena Football** team (www.azrattlers.com).

Participant Sports
Golf

The Phoenix area can rightfully claim to be the **golfing capital of the United States**. With over 170 courses in the Valley, it's simply golfing heaven. While golf here is generally expensive, keep in mind that **hotels often offer golfing packages** that get your price per round down to a more reasonable figure.

Some of the best public courses in the Valley include **The Boulders Resort Golf Club** north of Scottsdale in Carefree (www.theboulders.com); **The Phoenician Resort** between Scottsdale and the Camelback Corridor (www.thephoenician.com); the **TPC at Scottsdale** (www.tpc.com/daily/scottsdale) home of the FBR Open; **Troon North** in North Scottsdale (www.troonnorth.net), and **Grayhawk**, also in North Scottsdale (www.grayhawk.com).

Tennis is available at most hotels, especially the resorts, but many of the best players in the city play at the **Scottsdale Athletic Club & Resort**. (www.scottsdaleresortandathleticclub.com)

Hiking

There is so much great desert hiking in Phoenix that it's hard to narrow it down to the best. For a convenient in-town location try the many trails of the **Phoenix Mountain Preserve at Piestewa Peak** – formerly Squaw Peak — (http://phoenix.gov/PARKS/hikephx.html.) The **McDowell Sonoran Preserve** is a great escape in Scottsdale (http://www.scottsdaleaz.gov/preserve/trailsplan.asp), and the **South Mountain Preserve** in South Phoenix has tons of great trails as the largest municipal park in the country at over 16,000 acres (http://phoenix.gov/PARKS/hikesoth.html). Many visitors like the bragging rights that come from summiting **Camelback Mountain**, the highest spot in the city. (http://phoenix.gov/PARKS/hikecmlb.html)

Biking and Walking

Great **car-free biking and walking** can be found on both the Indian Bend Wash Greenbelt in Scottsdale and the canals of Scottsdale and Phoenix. The **Indian Bend Wash Greenbelt** roughly parallels Hayden Road in Scottsdale and connects parks and golf courses along a paved pathway. The **Arizona Canal Trails**, dirt paths that run along the city's canal system, are great for long runs and casual bike rides. Ask your hotel to point you to which ever is closer.

For **mountain biking,** you should check out the single track in the **parks mentioned in the hiking section,** as well as the out-standing competitive tracks at the **Estrella and McDowell Regional Parks**. (www.maricopa.gov/parks)

Horseback Riding

Wannabe wranglers can rent horses at the **Papago Riding Stables** in Papago Park in Tempe as well as at the **Ponderosa Stables** at South Mountain Park. (www.arizona-horses.com)

TUCSON BEST SHOPPING

Tucson has almost as many opportunities to shop for southwestern and Native American items as does Phoenix. There are also many wonderful galleries, boutiques, and even unique curio shops. If you just have to have national retailers, Tucson has malls too. **La Encantada Shopping Center** (www.westcor.com) features upscale shopping in the foothills of the Santa Catalinas. The **Tucson Mall** (www.tucsonmall.com), north of the University, is the largest and most centrally located. **Foothills Mall** (www.shopfoothills.com) on Ina Road in north Tucson just off of I-10 is also popular.

The **4ᵗʰ Avenue Shops** along Fourth Avenue between 4ᵗʰ and 7ᵗʰ Streets are great places to browse the day away. **Del Sol International Shops** (435 N 4ᵗʰ Ave) is a fantastic Indian and Southwestern store along 4ᵗʰ Ave. Another downtown locale of special interest to tourists is **El Mercado de Boutiques**, Broadway and Wilmot, which features Native American and Hispanic crafts. **Old Town Artisans** in the El Presidio Historic Park area may be the best place in town for Native American items.

Tucson doesn't have quite the concentration of **art galleries** that Scottsdale does, but among the best places are the galleries in the El Mercado shops, **Above & Below the Equator Gallery** at 521 4ᵗʰ Ave, and the already mentioned **Old Town Artisans**.

For one of a kind **furniture and outdoor items**, try the shops in the **Lost Barrio**, along Park Avenue just south of Broadway Blvd.

TUCSON BEST NIGHTLIFE

The downtown **Club Congress** (311 East Congress St., Tel. 520-622-8848) is known as THE place in town for cutting edge music and dancing. It's even been named one of the ten best rock clubs in the US. Across the street, the restored **Rialto Theater** (318 East Congress St., Tel. 520-740-1000) is wonderful spot to catch touring bands, comedians, and music festivals. East of the University, the **Cactus Moon Café** (5470 E Broadway, Tel. 520-748-0049) is a popular dance spot. The area around the University of Arizona has contemporary music and comedy clubs. Almost all of the resort hotels and many of the larger city hotels feature lounge entertainment.

The Tucson Arts District galleries stay upon until 7pm on the first and third Thursdays of the month, which is also when many shows open. It's a nice way to see the galleries and even sometimes meet the artists.

Tucson also has several supper clubs offering entertainment. For something different, try **El Mariachi Restaurant** (106 W Drachman, Tel. 520-791-7793). The Mexican cuisine is enhanced by the top-notch International Mariachi America group, which performs Wednesday-Sunday.

If **gambling** is your pleasure, you've got a couple of options. **Casino of the Sun** (7406 South Camino del Oeste, Tel. 520-883-1700) and **Desert Diamond Casino** (7350 South Nogales Highway, Tel. 520-294-7777) with both happily help you part with your money. Both are alcohol-free by the way.

You also have nice options for the **performing arts**. Tucson has a **Symphony Orchestra** (Tel. 520-882-8585, www.tucsonsymphony.org), the **Arizona Opera** (Tel. 520-293-4336, www.azopera.com), **Ballet Tucson** (520-903-1445, www.ballettucson.org), and the **Arizona Theater Company** (520-622-2823, www.aztheaterco.org). Check newspaper for listings and Ticketmaster (Tel. 520-321-1000) for tickets.

TUCSON BEST SPORTS & RECREATION

Spectator Sports
Baseball
Spring Training's Cactus League is a big hit in Tucson. The Arizona Diamondbacks, Colorado Rockies, and Chicago White Sox all have their spring training homes here (www.cactus-league.com). The **Arizona Heat**, a women's fast pitch team softball team, fills the baseball void here during the summer (www.arizonaprofastpitch.com).

The biggest spectator sport action in town focuses on the **University of Arizona Wildcats**. Perennial powerhouses in basketball, golf, baseball, softball and other sports, they are strongly supported by the local populous. Check the paper for events while you are in town. For information call Tel. 520-621-5130.

Participant Sports
Golf
While there aren't quite as many courses, golfing in Tucson can hold its own with Phoenix. Some excellent courses include both the mountain and canyon courses at the **Lodge at Ventana Canyon** (Tel. 520-577-4061), the **Randolph Municipal North Course** (Tel. 520-791-4336), the **Arizona National Golf Club** (Tel. 520-791-4336) and the **Silverbell Municipal Golf Course** (Tel. 520-791-4336.)

Tennis
Most of the major hotels and Tucson have courts and many allow non-guests to play for a higher fee. The following public tennis centers are also available: **Fort Lowell Park** (Tel. 520-791-2584), **Himmel Park** (Tel. 520-791-3276) and the **Randolph Tennis Center** (Tel. 520-791-4896.)

Hiking
There are many wonderful hiking opportunities in the Tucson area. See **Sabino Canyon** and both the East and West Sections of **Saguaro National Park** in the Tucson chapter for more information. Another great option when it's hot outside is **Mt. Lemmon**. With an altitude of over 9,000 feet, it's a place **to escape the heat during the summer months**. Take the ski lift up and then hike one of the many trails that lead off from the top of the lift (Tel. 520-576-1321).

Horseback Riding
The wonderful dude ranches around Tucson limit riding privileges to their overnight guests. Three stables along Oracle Road use trails in the Santa Catalina Mountains, providing a rural experience close to the city: **El Conquistador Stables** (Tel. 520-742-4200),

202 OPEN ROAD'S BEST OF ARIZONA

Pusch Ridge Stables (Tel. 520-825-1664), and **Walking Wind Stables** (Tel. 520-742-4422.)

Biking

Tucson is regularly named by *Bicycling Magazine* as **one of the top cities in the country for riding**. There are plenty of bike lanes and well as a couple of paved paths. You can download maps of both at www.pagnet.org/bikemap. The roads through both sections of Saguaro National Park are great rides through the giants of the desert, but avoid them during peak traffic times.

FLAGSTAFF BEST SHOPPING

There are many interesting **specialty shops and galleries in downtown Flagstaff**, most of these centered around **Aspen Avenue and San Francisco Street**. The **Museum of Northern Arizona** has a wonderful museum **gift shop** with outstanding Native American crafts as well as an **extensive bookstore**. Then there is always the **Flagstaff Mall** (www.westcor.com) out Highway 89 East.

FLAGSTAFF BEST NIGHTLIFE

Because Flagstaff is a college town, there are **plenty of bars and breweries that offer live music**. All you have to do is wander through the downtown historic district or along Beaver Street by campus and you'll find a happening spot. The **Beaver Street Brewery** and **Flagstaff Brewing Company** are always popular in the area, as is **San Felipe's Cantina**. More mature tipplers might prefer the **Wine Loft** downtown at 17 N. San Francisco Street. The **Museum Club** at 3404 East Route 66 is THE place for honky-tonkin' to live music.

Cultural events in Flagstaff are held in the 200-seat amphitheater of the **Coconino Center for the Arts**. (Tel. 928-779-6921, www.culturalpartners.org). The **Flagstaff Symphony Orchestra** is also active (Tel. 928-774-5107, www.flagstaffsymphony.org). The restored **Orpheum Theater** downtown (Tel. 928-556-1580, www.orpheumpresents.com) is a great place to catch **national touring acts**. **Theatrikos Theater Company** (Tel. 928-774-1662 , www.theatrikos.com) offers high-quality community theater productions.

Summer is a wonderful time in Flagstaff, with weekly **free concerts** on the square and in the park, salsa dancing on the square, and movie nights. Check the schedule at www.heritagesquaretrust.org.

FLAGSTAFF BEST SPORTS & RECREATION

Spectator Sports
The **Arizona Cardinals** hold their preseason training camp in **Flagstaff** at Northern Arizona University (www.flagstaff.az.us/phoenix_cardinals_training_camp.html). **Northern Arizona University** also has a full roster of NCAA sports in the **Big Sky Conference**. Check the local paper or http://nau.newtier.com/ for ticket information and schedules.

Participant Sports
Golf
There are some very nice golf courses that take advantage of the wonderful scenery in this part of the state. If you've never played at a higher altitude before, you'll love seeing your ball soar through the thinner mountain air. The only public course in **Flagstaff is the Elden Hills Golf Club** (Tel. 928-527-7997).

Hiking
In **Flagstaff** you can enjoy the numerous pine and aspen-shaded trails of the **Peaks District** of the **Coconino National Forest** (www.fs.fed.us/r3/coconino/recreation/peaks/rec_peaks.shtml.) If you take the road up to **Snowbowl** there are great hikes for every stamina level. The **Humphrey's Peak Trail**, difficult, summits the highest point in Arizona at 12,633 feet. The **Kachina Trail**, moderate, is one of the few trails that traverses the mountain instead of going straight up it, while the **Veit Springs Loop Trail**, easy, is a wonderful, kid-friendly walk through the aspens that includes a visit to an old homestead and views of pictographs.

Biking

There are mountain biking trails galore in Flagstaff. Beginners will enjoy the gravel FUTS **(Flagstaff Urban Trails System)** that has trails all over town. More experienced bikers need to make their way directly to the **Elden Trail System** north of town, where you'll find single track to your heart's content. You can rent bikes at **Absolute Bikes** (Tel. **928-779-5969,** 18 San Francisco St.).

Horseback Riding

If you'd like to spend some time in the saddle, there are plenty of options. Try **Hartman Outfitters** (www.hartmanoutfitters.com) just out of town or **High Mountain Stables** (www.highmountainstables.com) about 30 minutes away at Mormon Lake.

Snow Sports

Flagstaff is the place to go for wintertime fun. For downhill skiing and snowboarding **Arizona Snowbowl** (www.arizonasnowbowl.com) offers 32 runs off of four lifts. Cross-country skiers will enjoy the wonderful **Flagstaff Nordic Center** (www.flagstaffnordiccenter.com).

PRESCOTT BEST NIGHTLIFE

Whiskey Row, concentrated in the vicinity of Gurley and Montezuma Streets, is where you'll find the nightlife in Prescott. Check out **Matt's Saloon** and **The Palace**.

If you lean towards the fine arts, the **Prescott Fine Arts Association** (Tel. 928-445-3286, www.pfaa.net) stages plays, music and dance at its theater on Marina. Summer evenings see **performances held on Courthouse Plaza** (www.visit-prescott.com/event-calendar.html.)

For **gambling** you can hit **Bucky's Casino** (www.buckyscasino.com) on the way into Prescott on Highway 69. Otherwise you'll have to do some driving to visit the **Cliff Castle Casino** (Tel. 928-567-7900) in Camp Verde at exit 289 off I-17.

PRESCOTT BEST SPORTS & RECREATION

Hiking

Prescott hikes often lead to **awe-inspiring granite formations**. The **Granite Basin Recreation Area** has a wonderful system of trails that range from easy to difficult. **Thumb Butte**, a distinctive Prescott rock formation, also has a trail that leads up to and over its shoulder.

Horseback Riding

Smokin' Gun Adventures (Tel. 928-778-9154) will get you out on the trail like Prescott's cowboys of old.

SEDONA BEST SHOPPING & NIGHTLIFE

Sedona is full of shopping opportunities. There are **galleries and shops along 89A on the main drag** of town as well as at the **Tlaquepaque Village** on 179 right before the Y. For discounts, try the **Factory Outlet Stores** on 179 at the Village of Oak Creek.

The Sedona nightlife concentrates in **bars and brewpubs** in the heart of town. The **Oak Creek Brewing Company** (Tel. 928-204-1300) has live music on weekends. **The Sedona Arts Center** (www.sedonaartscenter.com) hosts various cultural events.

SEDONA BEST SPORTS & RECREATION

Golf

Sedona has a number of good courses, but the **Sedona Golf Resort** (Tel. 800-426-6148) is especially beautiful. The par 3 hole #10 stands out as one of the most photographed holes in Arizona.

Hiking

Sedona has more wonderful trails that there is space to mention here. Located in the **Red Rock District** of the **Coconino National Forest** (www.fs.fed.us/r3/coconino/recreation/red_rock/rec_redrock.shtml), the town boasts great hiking in every direction. The **Courthouse Loop**, moderate, located between Sedona and the Village of Oak Creek, is one of my favorites for first-time visitors. **Boyton Canyon**, an easy hike along a vortex site, is also very popular. The **Devil's Bridge** trail, moderate, leads to the largest sandstone arch in the Sedona area.

Biking
Although not as famous for biking as the slick rock of Moab, Sedona has some of its own **sick slick rock**. Advanced riders will love the **Broken Arrow Loop**, between the Village of Oak Creek and Sedona, while beginners should enjoy the easy **Bell Rock Pathway** in the same area. Rentals at **Absolute Bikes** (Tel. 877-284-1242, 6101 Highway 179 in the Village of Oak Creek.)

Horseback Riding
You can go with **Trail Horse Adventures** to see the red rock from the back of a horse (www.trailhorseadventures.com) .

Jeep Tours
Probably the most popular **Sedona** adventure, jeep tours are easy to arrange and fun to take. Check out the original operator, **Pink Jeep Tours** (www.pinkjeep.com, Tel. 800-873-3662), or the supposedly more eco-conscious **Hummer Affair** (www. Hummeraffair.com, Tel. 928-282-6656).

GRAND CANYON BEST SHOPPING

All of the hotels and stores in the Grand Canyon offer souvenirs that range from silly t-shirts to wonderful works of art by Native American craftsmen. The **gift shop at El Tovar** on the South Rim is one of the nicer ones, while the one at the **Bright Angel Lodge** has an extensive array of items.

If you are headed from the South Rim to the North Rim, you will pass a number of **trading posts**, all of which carry Native American crafts. The largest and best of these is the **Cameron Trading Post**. With a large gift shop and wonderful gallery, they have it all. If you can't find a gift here, then it probably isn't made. (www.camerontradingpost.com., 54 miles north of Flagstaff on Highway 89)

GRAND CANYON BEST NIGHTLIFE

Watching the sunset or listening to the crickets isn't the only way to pass the evening while at the Grand Canyon. There are, surprisingly, a number of other options. Bright Angel, El Tovar, and Mazwik Lodges on the South Rim all have occasional entertainment in their **lounges**. In addition, there are various programs throughout the year at the **Shrine of the Ages Theater** located adjacent to the Visitor Center, including a fantastic music festival in September (www.grandcanyonmusicfest.org).

GRAND CANYON BEST SPORTS & RECREATION

Biking
Bikes are allowed on all paved roads and other areas designated as bike accessible. There are, however, no rentals, so you'll have to bring your own bike if you intend to ride. Be aware that the road has very little shoulder and traffic can be quite heavy.

South Rim Hiking
Hiking is the main draw as far as recreation in the canyon goes. Most of the hikes on the South Rim, with the exception of the **Rim Trail**, are steep and strenuous. If you are hiking down to the river, it's nice to descend along the ridge of the **South Kaibab Trail** and

ascend via the **Bright Angel Trail**. The **Grandview Trail**, which does not go down to the river, is a nice out and back to Horseshoe Mesa.

North Rim Hiking
There are a handful of level trails on the North Rim. The **Bright Angel Point Trail** is a short (1/2 mile) trail out to a wonderful lookout area. The **Cape Final Trail**, about three miles roundtrip, offers wonderful rim views, as does the **Transept Trail**. The **North Kaibab Trail** leads into the canyon from the North Rim.

Backcountry Hiking

If you want to overnight in the canyon, you **must get a backcountry permit**. You can request a permit by mail (Backcountry Office Grand Canyon National Park, P.O. Box 129, Grand Canyon, Arizona 86023) or fax (Tel. 928-638-2125), but not by phone. You can request permits up to four months in advance. If you have questions, you can call the backcountry office at Tel. 928-638-7888 or check out their website at www.nps.gov/grca/backcountry. You can rent camping equipment on the South Rim at Babbitt's General Store (Tel. 928-638-2854).

Mule Trips and Tours

Mule trips are a very popular way to see the canyon, so it is suggested that **reservations be made six to eight months in advance**. There are three different trips. One is an overnight trip to the Phantom Ranch, while another is a three-day journey. The last, a **one-day trip, is the most popular**. Departing daily from both the North and South Rims, it descends over 3,000 feet to the canyon's Tonto Platform (not all the way to the Colorado River.) The round-trip takes about seven hours. Tel. 888-297-2757. www.grandcanyonlodges.com/Mule-Trips-716.html. $135 for one-day trip. Rider qualifications include weight limit (200 pounds), height limit (must be at least 4'7") and English fluency.

Horseback Riding

As of the writing of this edition, the only providers of horseback rides in the park, Apache Stables, had closed. No other companies have stepped in yet to fill the void.

Rafting

Rafting the Colorado River through the Grand Canyon is an unforgettable experience. Both smooth and white water trips are offered. The **smooth water trips** take about 12 hours and include round-trip bus transportation from the Grand Canyon Village. You'll **float from the Glen Canyon Dam** outside of Page, Arizona to Lee's Ferry, where the park officially starts. Call Aramark-Wilderness River Adventures (Tel. 928-645-3279) for reservations and information. You may also make arrangements through Grand Canyon National Park Lodges for transportation from the South Rim to Page. Call 303-297-2757 for more information.

Whitewater rafting on the Colorado is one of the world's great experiences. Although a few operators offer trips as short as three days, the majority of Grand Canyon rafting adventures are between six and nine days long. The season usually runs from April through October. You can contact the park office for a list of concessionaires (www.nps.gov/grca/river/, Tel. 928-638-7843). Plan on making your reservations far in advance if you wish to experience the canyon in this manor.

Grand Canyon

Northeastern Arizona

Cross-Country Skiing

There are no groomed trails, but you are free to cross-country ski as conditions permit. Ski rentals are available at Babbitt's General Store in the Grand Canyon Village (Tel. 928-638-2854).

NORTHEASTERN ARIZONA BEST SHOPPING

Navajo Nation Shopping

Both the **gift shops at the lodges** as well as the numerous **trading posts** in the region offer Native American jewelry, crafts, rugs and mementos. The **Hubbell Trading Post** is one of the best. You'll even find crafts for sale deep in the canyon at the White House ruins in Canyon de Chelly.

Hopi Reservation Shopping

The **Hopi Cultural Center** has an outstanding collection of **all kinds of Hopi crafts**. *Info*: Tel 928-734-6650. Highway AZ-264. Open 8am-5pm weekdays and 9am-3pm on weekends. $3 Adults. $1 children under 13.

NORTHEASTERN ARIZONA BEST NIGHTLIFE

Of all the areas in Arizona, the northeast has the least in the way of nightlife. Composed mainly of small towns and Indian reservations, your best bet will be the hotel lounges. Remember, there is no alcohol allowed on the Indian reservations.

NORTHEASTERN ARIZONA BEST SPORTS & RECREATION

Navajo Nation Hiking

Most hiking on the reservation must be done with a guide. The exceptions to this are the wonderful **White House Ruins Trail** at Canyon de Chelly, and the **Wildcat Trail** in Monument Valley.

If you want to hike with a guide, the **Betatakin** and **Keet Seel** hikes at the **Navajo National Monument** are phenomenal. You can also take guided hikes into **Canyon de Chelly** and **Monument Valley**.

Navajo Nation Horseback Riding

Horseback riding can be arranged at both Canyon del Chelly and Monument Valley. Your hotel will be able to help you make arrangements, or, in the off-season, you can just show up the day before and arrange it yourself.

Lake Powell Boating

Almost any kind of boat, power or sail, is allowed and available for rental. Be aware, however, that small boats can be dangerous during storms when Lake Powell can become rather turbulent.

House boating is an extremely popular way to experience Lake Powell. The boats are available for rent all over Page, but the easiest to coordinate is probably with the Lake Powell Resort at the Wahweap Marina (Tel. 800-528-6154, www.lakepowell.com.) All boats, regardless of size, feature walkways, range, oven, refrigerator, ice chest, heater, shower, toilet, charcoal grill, and bunk-style beds. All necessary supplies, including a full tank of gas, are furnished to you except that you must provide your own bedding, linens and food. They don't require any special skills or prior boating experience except for an understanding of basic boating rules and courtesy. Be sure to buy a detailed map of the lake at the time of rental.

Lake Powell Fishing

Bass, trout, and crappie are all popular catches in Lake Powell. An Arizona fishing license is required. You may also be required to have a Utah fishing license if fishing from a boat. You can secure both locally.

Lake Powell Rafting

You can experience a float trip down a smooth portion of the Colorado River. You'll travel on the river through beautiful sandstone cliffs from the Glen Canyon Dam to Lee's Ferry, the official start of the Grand Canyon. Check out **Wilderness River Adventures** (www.riveradventures.com, Tel. 928-645-3279) for more information.

Lake Powell Water Sports

Swimmers will find beaches in the Wahweap area and through-out the lake. Water skiing is done mainly in the wider channels and bays of the lake. Be alert for marked areas where water skiing is prohibited.

EASTERN ARIZONA BEST SHOPPING & NIGHTLIFE

There are antique and craft shops to poke around in both Greer and Pinetop. Stores in Holbrook and Winslow carry some nice quality Native American-made goods.

Some of the larger hotels in the region have live music during busy seasons, but in reality the nightlife in this area is pretty sparse. There are a number of **casinos** however, including the **Apache Gold Casino** outside of Globe (www.apachegoldcasinoresort.com, Tel. 800-272-2438), the **Mazatzal Casino** in Payson (www.777play.com, Tel. 800-777-7529), the **Hon Dah Casino** outside of Pinetop (www.hon-dah.com, Tel. 800-929-8744).

EASTERN ARIZONA BEST SPORTS & RECREATION

Fishing

There are numerous lakes for fishing in the White Mountains. Try the Bunch, River, and Tunnel Lakes around Greer; Fred's Lake, 1/4 mile south of AZ 260 between Hon-Dah and Pinetop; or Rainbow Lake, off AZ 260 in Lakeside. The Little Colorado River in Greer is also a fisherman's delight.

Golf

There are plenty of public courses in the region. Try the **Alpine Country Club** (Tel. 928-339-4944) in Alpine; the **Payson Golf Club** (Tel. 928- 474-2273) in Payson; or the **Pinetop Lakes Golf and Country Club** in Pinetop (Tel. 928-369-4531). The **Silver Creek Golf Club** near Show Low a Golf Digest 4-star course (928-537-2744.)

Hiking

There is wonderful hiking all over Eastern Arizona. Near Holbrook, the **Petrified Forest National Park** has a series of trails that wind through the incredible colored stone stumps.

In the White Mountains **near Greer**, you can climb Mt Baldy, the second highest peak in the state, or Escudilla Mountain, the third highest, or just enjoy the intricate series of trails strewn through out the **Apache-Sitgreaves National Forest** (www.fs.fed.us/r3/asnf/recreation/trails/)

Hannagan Meadow abuts the **Blue Range Primitive Area**, where you can literally hike for days and not see the same area twice. (www.fs.fed.us/r3/asnf/recreation/trails/alpine_trails/index.shtml.)

Pinetop-Lakeside has the **White Mountains Trail System**, which is a series of 11 loop trails in the Lakeside Ranger District. (www.ci.pinetop-lakeside.az.us/trailsystem.shtml.)

There are plenty of **hikes around Payson** as well. They range from the one-mile loop at the Tonto Natural Bridge State Park to the 51-mile Highline Trail. (www.arizonahikingtrails.com/paysonhikes.asp.)

Horseback Riding

If you want to explore the area on horseback, there are plenty of good options. In Greer call the **X Diamond Ranch** (Tel. 928-333-2286); in Hannagan Meadow arrange ahead with the **Hannagan Meadow Stables** (Tel. 928-339-4370) and in the Pinetop-Lakeside area try the **Thunderhorse Ranch** (Tel. 928-368-5593).

Skiing

Sunrise Park Resort, 15 minutes from Greer and 35 minutes from Pinetop-Lakeside, offers the most consistent snow in the state as they have **snow-making facilities**. With 65 runs, a terrain park for snowboarders, a Ski-Wee area for the kids, and cross-country skiing, there is something for everyone (www.sunriseskipark.com, Tel. 800-772-7669).

WESTERN ARIZONA BEST SHOPPING

Lake Havasu

The **English Village** at the foot of the London Bridge is the place for shopping. There are over 40 stores located there, as well as restaurants, entertainment, and activities.

Wickenburg

Pick up the perfect western outfit at **Double D Western Wear**, 955 W. Wickenburg Way, Tel. 928-684-7987. **North Tenger** and **Frontier** streets also have a number of western wear stores as well as small shops and galleries.

WESTERN ARIZONA BEST NIGHTLIFE

Bullhead City/Laughlin, Nevada

People come here to gamble. In Laughlin you can find Vegas-imported casinos such as the **Golden Nugget, Harrah's**, and the **Flamingo**. Or, for that whole Mississippi River vibe, try the **Colorado Belle**. All are located on the Nevada side of the Colorado River, which is Laughlin's "strip" if you will.

Lake Havasu

The nightlife in Lake Havasu can be found in the **lounges and bars** along the waterfront and in the London Bridge area. Two good bets are **Kokomo's** on Queen's Bay Road (Tel. 928-855-8782) or **Chili Charlie's** at 790 N Lake Havasu Ave, Tel. 928-453-5055.

214 OPEN ROAD'S BEST OF ARIZONA

WESTERN ARIZONA BEST SPORTS & RECREATION

Western
Arizona

WESTERN ARIZONA BEST SPORTS & RECREATION

Lake Havasu

Even if you don't have a watercraft, you can enjoy the lake at one of the city's public beaches. Try **London Bridge Beach**, on the island across from London Bridge; **Rotary Beach Park**, south of the bridge; and **Lake Havasu State Park** north of the bridge.

People come to Lake Havasu to enjoy the lake. **Boat tours** are a very popular option here. Try **Blue Water Jet Boat Tours** for a two-hour trip up the Colorado River. (Tel. 888-855-717. www.coloradoriverjetboattours.com.) **Western Arizona Canoe & Kayak Outfitters** rents all sorts of self-propelled watercraft (Tel. 888-881-5038. www.azwacko.com). **Ski boats and jet skis** can be rented from **Action Adventure Rentals in the English Village (Tel.** 928-854-5377, www.actionadventurerentals.com).

There's golf to be had in Lake Havasu as well. Try the **London Bridge Golf Club** (Tel. 928-855-2719) with two 18-hole championship courses; or the 9-hole executive course at the **London Bridge Resort** (Tel. 928-855-4777.)

Wickenburg

Most people come to Wickenburg for the dude ranches, so obviously **horseback riding** is a popular option here. Day visitors who aren't staying at a dude ranch can rent horses at **Effus Land & Cattle Company**, Tel. 928-671-0381, or **Polly Anne's Wickenburg Stables**, Tel. 928-684-7331.

Golfers can hit the links at the Los Caballeros Golf Club, which is part of the Los Caballeros dude ranch (Tel. 928-684-2704, www.sunc.com/golf.html).

Jeep tours with **BC Jeep Tours** (Tel. 928-684-7901) are another fun way to see the countryside.

13. PRACTICAL
MATTERS

Airports/Arrivals
Arizona's busiest air-
port and the one with
the greatest choice of
airlines and flights is
Phoenix's **Sky Harbor
International Airport**.
However, if you're go-
ing to be concentrating
on the southern part of
the state the airport in Tucson is a good secondary choice.

Two major airlines have important hubs in Phoenix. These are **US
Air** (formerly **America West**), which is headquartered here, and
discount maverick **Southwest Airlines**. Both of them have more
non-stop destinations from Phoenix than any other airline. Check
them first.

These are the main carriers serving Phoenix:
• **Alaska Airlines**, Tel. 800/426-0333, www.alaskaair.com
• **American**, Tel. 800/433-7300, www.aa.com
• **America West/US Air**, Tel. 800/235-9292, www.americawest.com
• **Continental**, Tel. 800/523-0280, www.continental.com
• **Delta Airlines**, Tel. 800/221-1212, www.delta.com
• **Hawaiian Airlines**, Tel. 800/367-5320, www.hawaiianair.com
• **Northwest Airlines,** Tel. 800/225-2525, www.nwa.com:
• **Southwest Airlines**, Tel. 800/435-9792, www.southwest.com:
• **United Airlines**, Tel. 800/241-6522, www.unitedl.com:
• **US Airways,** Tel. 800/428-4322, www.usair.com

International service, available from American, US Air / America West, Continental and United, is also provided by several foreign airlines. These are **AeroMexico, Air Canada, British Airways** and **Lufthansa**.

Tucson International Airport is much smaller and handles far fewer flights, although a number of the same airlines that serve Phoenix can also take you to Tucson. They are **Alaska, American, America West/US Air, Continental, Delta, Skywest (Delta Connection and United Express), Southwest, Northwest,** and **United**.

Both the Phoenix and Tucson airports offer **straightforward arrivals** to the city. There are cabs, shuttle services, hotel courtesy vans, and city buses at curbside as you exit the baggage claim area. The Phoenix airport has one central terminal for all car rentals that is accessed by a curbside bus. In Tucson the car rental companies have cars in a garage adjacent to the main terminal.

Getting Around
By Air
Almost all air travel within Arizona is provided by the **Mesa Air Group**, Tel. 800/MESA-AIR, www.mesa-air.com. They operate in Arizona as **America West Express** and their flights can also be booked in conjunction with flights to other parts of the country on America West. In addition to Phoenix, Mesa Air serves Bullhead City, Flagstaff, Sierra Vista (near Tucson), Kingman, Lake Havasu City, and Yuma. They also have flights to a number of locations in southern and central California. **Scenic Airlines**, Tel. 800/634-6801, www.scenic.com, isn't so much a carrier as it is a tour operator. Their base is in Las Vegas and they offer day and overnight trips to both the Grand Canyon and Monument Valley in Arizona.

Car Rental
A car, whether it's your own or a rental, is **definitely the best way to get around** in Arizona. Besides being the most time and cost effective method, it also offers the traveler a degree of flexibility that cannot be matched by any form of public transportation. If you from another country and plan to rent a car, be sure to have a valid **International Drivers License**.

Major Car Rental Agencies in Phoenix & Tucson

	Toll Free	Phoenix	Tucson
Alamo, www.alamo.com	800/462-5266	602/244-0897	520/573-4740
Avis, www.avis.com	800/230-4898	602/273-3222	520/294-1494
Budget, www.budget.com	800/527-0700	602/267-1717	520/889-8800
Dollar, www.dollar.com	800/800-3665	602/275-7588	520/573-8486
Enterprise www.enterprise.com	800/325-8007	602/225-0588	520/295-1964
Hertz, www.hertz.com	800/654-3131	602/267-8822	520/294-7616
National www.nationalcar.com	800/227-7368	602/275-4771	520/573-8050
Thrifty, www.thrifty.com	800/847-4389	602/244-0311	520/790-2277

Good driving maps of Arizona are available from AAA and major bookstores. The map put out by the Office of Tourism is also an acceptable source. If you wait until your arrival in Arizona, you can purchase road maps at the Phoenix and Tucson airports.

Train Travel

Like most of the western and mountain states, Arizona caters to the car driver. For those willing to put up with the inconvenience of public transportation, here's some guidance on getting around from one city to another by train.

Amtrak, Tel. 800-USA-RAIL; www.amtrak.com, serves a number of Arizona communities. The daily Southwest Chief (Chicago to Los Angeles) traverses the north-central portion of the state from east to west and has stops at Winslow, Flagstaff, and Kingman. Connecting bus service from Flagstaff is available to both the Grand Canyon and Phoenix. In the south, two separate trains serve Benson, Tucson, Maricopa, and Yuma. Each of these trains, the Sunset Limited (Florida to Los Angeles) and the Texas Eagle (Chicago to Los Angeles), runs three times a week. From Tucson there is connecting bus service to Phoenix.

The state does have four excellent "tourist" train trips:

• **The Grand Canyon Railway**: Passengers ride in carefully restored coaches that recreate the atmosphere of 1901 when service to the Grand Canyon was inaugurated. Vintage locomotives add to the authenticity of the 2-1/4 hour trip from Williams to the South Rim. You'll arrive at a depot that was built in 1910 and is the only log railroad station still in use in the nation. Visitors have about 3-1/2 hours of sight seeing time along the South Rim before the train returns to Williams, which is accessible from Phoenix via bus. (www.thetrain.com, Tel. 800-843-8724)

• **San Pedro and Southwestern Railway**: Leaving from Benson (about 45 miles east of Tucson), the San Pedro and Southwestern rides through an historic section of southern Arizona. The four-hour excursion passes through old mining and ghost towns and includes a western barbecue lunch during a stop in Tombstone. Benson is served by bus from Tucson. (Tel. 520-586-2266)

• **Verde Canyon Railway**: The Verde Canyon Railway travels through a scenic portion of the Verde Canyon and Sycamore Wilderness that cannot be reached by road. The trip departs from Clarkdale, which is only a few miles from Sedona. The four-hour journey offers thrilling trestles that span deep canyons as well as views of ancient Indian ruins. Bus service is available to Sedona. You need a car or taxi to get to Clarkdale. (www.verdecanyonrr.com, 800-320-0718)

• **Yuma Valley Railway**: This shorter (two hour) trip travels along the Colorado River and goes into neighboring California as well as the Mexican states of Sonora and Baja California. Passenger coaches date from the 1920s while the locomotives are from the '40s or '50s. Yuma is served by bus and Amtrak. (Tel. 928-782-9629)

Taxis
Although Phoenix and Tucson are large, cosmopolitan cities, you won't be able to hail a cab on the street except for at the airport. You'll have to have your hotel call one for you. In smaller cities, the cab service is even spottier, although it does exist in medium-sized towns like Flagstaff and Sedona.

Bus
Bus service is provided by **Greyhound**, Tel. 800/231-2222 (for route information and reservations). Their website is www.greyhound.com. Within the large Navajo Indian Reservation there is regularly scheduled bus service along several different routes. This low-cost service (about 8 cents per mile) is provided by the **Navajo Transit System**, Tel. 928/729-4002. They have seven routes serving all of the region's major communities. It operates Monday through Friday only.

Business Hours
As is the case in much of the US, businesses are staying open later and later to accommodate busy schedules. Banks and govern-

ment offices are generally still only open from 9-5. Museums often have one night a week that they stay open later than usual.

Climate & Weather

Many people have the mistaken impression that Arizona is hot and dry all the time from one corner of the state to another. But, like everything else you'll encounter here, variation is the name of the game. Yes, many parts of the state have blistering arid summers and mild dry winters. However, winter is a very literal term for northern Arizona where heavy snow provides great skiing near Flagstaff and closes roads to the North Rim of the Grand Canyon for several months of the year. Therefore, the best time to visit Arizona depends upon what areas of the state you're going to be concentrating on and what outdoor activities you're planning.

The **northern portion of the state**, roughly corresponding to the Colorado Plateau region has mild to warm summers and cold winters. Precipitation comes mostly in the form of summertime thundershowers and some significant winter snowstorms. If you plan to spend all or most of your Arizona vacation in the north, the months from May through September are best.

The remainder of the state is mostly dry and hot in the summer. Temperatures in the desert sizzle during the day, especially in the **Phoenix** area and along the western edge of the state around Yuma. **Tucson** is a few degrees cooler and even that small variance can make quite a difference in comfort levels.

For a sightseeing vacation, the fall through winter is a better time to visit than the middle of summer. However, if you're coming to Arizona mainly to stay at a resort and sit by the pool, keep in mind that desert winters aren't like those in Florida – the heart of winter is often too cool to fully enjoy those types of activities – early spring or fall would be more appropriate.

A vacation that cuts across all parts of the state is also well suited to the less extreme weather conditions present in the fall or spring. However, it's probably much wiser to contend with the summer heat than risk not being able to get somewhere in the winter because of a heavy snow.

Temperature & Rainfall Averages

Temperature Highs/Lows & Annual Precipitation

	Jan.	April	July	Oct.	Precip.
Flagstaff	41/14	57/27	81/50	63/31	19.8"
Grand Canyon	41/17	59/30	83/52	64/34	13.1"
Kingman	57/31	75/42	97/67	79/47	10.7"
Page	45/23	67/38	94/63	71/42	10.2"
Phoenix	65/38	84/52	105/77	88/57	7.0"
Prescott	51/23	69/38	91/61	74/42	15.4"
Tucson	63/38	81/50	98/74	84/56	11.0"
Yuma	68/43	86/57	106/81	90/62	3.2"

Electricity
AC, 110 volts/60 cycles.

Emergencies & Safety
In any emergency situation you should **dial 911** for coordinated assistance. All of Arizona is on this system and your call will be automatically routed to the nearest emergency service.

Safety concerns are no greater or less here than other parts of the country. Don't leave items lying around exposed in your car, even for a short time, and use lockboxes at hotels for valuables.

Festivals & Holidays
Arizona observes all national holidays.

Notable events include the **Rodeo Parade** in Tucson in February; **Cinco de Mayo** events around the state in May; **Frontier Days** in Prescott in June; **Independence Day** celebrations around the state in July; the **Coconino Country Fair** in Flagstaff in August; the **Navajo Nation Fair** in Window Rock in September; the **Arizona State Fair** in Phoenix in October; and **Christmas lights and festivities** all over the state in December.

Telephones/Area Codes
Greater Phoenix has three area codes – 602 for the Central Valley, 480 for the East Valley, and 623 for the West Valley. Tucson and cities south are in area code 520. North of Phoenix is all area code 928.

You might want to keep in mind that most of Arizona, outside the Navajo Nation, does not observe daylight savings time. So, even if you are calling within the 928 area code, you might be calling to another time zone.

Time
Although all of Arizona is on **Mountain Time** (two hours earlier than the east coast and one hour later than the west coast), things get complicated for two reasons. First of all, Arizona is one of the few places in the country that **does not observe Daylight Savings Time**. As a result, when most places are observing Daylight Savings Time, Arizona isn't, making it the same as Pacific Time. BUT, the **Navajo Nation does observe Daylight Savings Time**. So, when you are going somewhere like Monument Valley or Canyon del Chelly during the summer, it will be a different time there than it is in the rest of Arizona.

Tipping
It is standard to tip 15% at restaurants on the total bill for meals (before tax), 10% for taxis, and $1-2 a day for maid service. And of course, if people provide exceptionally good service or go out of their way for you, a more generous tip is often given. Keep in mind that most people who are employed in the tourist industry, specifically hotels and restaurants, don't get great salaries. They count on tips for a significant part of their income.

Tourist Information
The Arizona Office of Tourism (www.arizonaguide.com) can supply you with a general state visitor's guide as well as numerous other brochures, special publications and maps. If you don't have access to the internet, you can call their toll-free telephone information line Tel. 888-520-3434 or 602-230-7733. More specific information on cities and regions is available from local chambers of commerce or visitor bureaus.

Websites
There are hundreds of internet sites devoted either exclusively or partially to Arizona and traveling in the state. Some of the more important statewide sites are listed here. Many localities have their own site as well.

• **www.arizonaguide.com**: This is the official website of the Arizona Office of Tourism and an extensive one with state-wide information and many links.

• **www.recreation.gov:** Covers areas managed by all federal agencies including the all-important National Parks Service.

• **www.state.az.us**: Official site of Arizona's state government. It has information on all aspects of Arizona, including tourism and lodging reservations.

INDEX

Things Change!

Phone numbers, prices, addresses, quality of service – all change. If you come across any new information, we'd appreciate hearing from you. No item is too small! Drop us an e-mail at jopenroad@aol.com, visit us at www.openroadguides.com, or write us at:

Open Road's Best of Arizona
Open Road Publishing
P.O. Box 284
Cold Spring Harbor, NY 11724

Travel Notes

About the Author

Becky Youman first lived in Arizona as a graduate student, where she took advantage of not having class on Fridays and explored the state every weekend. She moved back years later with her family and now calls both Scottsdale and Flagstaff home. She is a freelance writer whose other titles include Open Road's *Chile Guide* and *Ecuador & Galapagos Islands Guide*. Her most recent book, *Liquid Mexico*, is a travelogue that delves into the festivities and history related to Mexico's most famous libations.

The New Open Road Travel Guides

Open Road has launched a radical new concept in travel guides: matching the time you *really* have for your vacation with the right amount of information you need for your perfect trip! No fluff, just the best things to do and see, the best places to stay and eat. Includes one-day, weekend, one-week and two-week trip ideas. It's the *perfect* travel guide!

Open Road's Best of Costa Rica, $14.95
Open Road's Best of Honduras, $14.95
Open Road's Best of Las Vegas, $14.95
Open Road's Best of Arizona, $14.95
Open Road's Best of Ireland, $14.95

And look for new guides to California, Italy, Belize, The Bahamas, The Caribbean and more in 2007.

Family Travel
Italy with Kids, $16.95
Paris with Kids, $16.95
Caribbean with Kids, $14.95
London with Kids, $14.95
New York City with Kids, $14.95
National Parks With Kids, $14.95
L.A. with Kids, $14.95
Washington, DC with Kids, $14.95
Hawaii with Kids, $14.95

Menu Translators
Eating & Drinking in Paris, $9.95
Eating & Drinking in Italy, $9.95
Eating & Drinking in Spain, $9.95

Made Easy Sights & Walks Guides
New York City Made Easy, $9.95
San Francisco Made Easy, $9.95
Amsterdam Made Easy, $9.95
Berlin Made Easy, $9.95
Dublin Made Easy, $9.95
Europe Made Easy, $10.95
Florence Made Easy, $9.95
Paris Made Easy, $9.95
Provence Made Easy, $9.95
Rome Made Easy, $9.95
Venice Made Easy, $9.95

Order now at
www.openroadguides.com